No Splits

Can you trust God with
the whole of your life?

Steve Shaw

Marshall Pickering

Marshall Morgan and Scott
Marshall Pickering
34–42 Cleveland Street, London, W1P 5FB. U.K.

First published in 1989 by Marshall Morgan and Scott
Publications Ltd
Part of the Marshall Pickering Holdings Group

British Library Cataloguing in Publication Data
Shaw, Steve
   No splits: can you trust God with the whole of your
life?
   1. Christian life. Spirituality
   248.4

   ISBN 0 551 01884 4

Text set in Bembo by Watermark, Hampermill Cottage,
Watford WD1 4PL.
Printed in Great Britain by Courier International,
Tiptree, Colchester

Contents

'We must give up the childish fantasy of becoming saints in favour of the altogether loftier, more demanding and nobler task of becoming human beings.'

Dietrich Bonhoeffer

Acknowledgments

I would like to thank James Olthuis, Hendrik Hart, Paul Marshall and Calvin Seerveld, friends and professors at the Institute for Christian Studies, Toronto, and John Peck, the head of College House. These five have profoundly influenced my thinking and much of the content of this book. None of them, I hasten to add, is responsible for any nonsense that may appear in what follows. I would also like to thank my friends from the Greenbelt Festival and College House who have, over the years, struggled with me to put into practice the perspective I have put forward in this book. Lastly I would like to thank Jo Wroe for editing the manuscipt and John Chaplin and Ed Wall for reading and commenting on parts of it.

Foreword

I've been looking forward to this book.

It's not simply that Steve Shaw is a good friend and very likely to write a good book. It's not even just that he has a lot of insight. It's also that Steve has his own inimitable style in opening up the Christian faith for other people. He communicates in a way which can take people off their guard, coming out sometimes with surprises and sometimes with conclusions which are more familiar and comfortable, yet always in a way that is challenging and authentic.

The book is in fact a sort of journey into ourselves. For even though we all take ourselves quite seriously we rarely reflect on who we are or the way we see things. So the theme running through Steve's book is that because of this lack of self-reflection we accept much which comes from pagan and secular roots. And for the Christian, as well as for others, the result is to create splits and tensions in ourselves which are destructive and hurtful. It is Steve Shaw's aim to open up for us a way of living and thinking where there are No Splits.

It's an ambitious aim, but as we read on we become convinced that it is a realisable one. One of the first splits Steve touches on is the war between body and soul, flesh and spirit, emotions and intellect. These he traces back to the influence of Plato and earlier Greek myths, which have been taken into Christianity.

Yet stories or myths are not simply to be discounted. They are often the deepest expression of our answers to the biggest questions of life. They are also answers which we absorb from our society as easily as we breathe. The answers can be founded on Christian truth or be derived from some other source, but whichever they are we hold them by faith. The recognition that the whole world lives by faith is implicit in Steve's analysis. The crucial question is where that faith lies.

The faith offered throughout the book is that in the Creator, Redeemer God, revealed to us in Jesus Christ. It is in God that our meaning and our integration is to be found. Yet again, the choice is not between serving God and living autonomously. The option is always one of service – either of the true God or an idol. And here we see the futility of choosing an idol spelled out for us so well. For wherever our faith lies, the whole creation continues to speak God's glory, and not even the pagan ruler can avoid addressing this great theme in one way or another.

Living without splits before God means that we need no longer suppress areas of our lives, but God can open them up in fulness. For our God is a God who shows us how to love ourselves as well as others, a God of the emotions, of aesthetics, of justice. This is a God of song, art and dance, of celebration and feasts. The call is always to serve this God and to know ourselves in God's world. The alternative is to live our denials, to reconstitute justice through partial models, and to shape our own style by our idols.

I hope you'll enjoy this book, and be drawn by its vision. Because Steve Shaw offers his readers a God who is involved both in our fasting and in our dinner parties, and a life which can be lived in joy, but also with tears. It is a life of integrity, wholeness and fulness; one where we are not constantly torn in two or serving two rulers, but one focused on the living God in whom we do not need to live divided lives.

ELAINE STORKEY
London 1989

Introduction

If we are serious about our Christian faith then we know that we are called to serve God with 'every fibre of our being'. In the past we responded to this call by entering certain professions that we identified as 'full-time service for God'. To become a minister or to join a missionary organisation was at the top of our list. If for some reason we felt that these options were not open to us, we settled for 'subordinate' ones and became nurses, doctors or social workers or entered one of the other caring professions.

Many of us, however, were well entrenched in 'more worldly' professions when we became Christians. Although the pull to 'full-time Christian work' was often great we felt that the upheaval would be too big and, after all, we were happy in our present work. We decided we would serve the Lord just where we were. Our workplace would be our mission field. Our missionary enterprise consisted of two main aims: to uphold impeccable standards in personal moral behaviour (or at least to hide our moral shortcomings!) and to take every opportunity to evangelise. This we understood mainly in terms of saving souls for heaven. Many of us found that the results were disappointing. We alienated our work mates from ourselves and our gospel. Not to be defeated we sought to do the 'Lord's work' outside working hours: we led the Bible study group and involved ourselves in every church activity that was on offer.

Over the past two decades, a new generation of Christians has emerged to challenge these traditional ways of serving God. They have rejected what seemed to them a Christianity that is narrowly moralistic and (because it focuses on what happens to us when we die) is out of touch with the concerns of this world. These 'modernists' have insisted that to serve the Lord does not mean that we must choose certain professions and activities as 'spiritual' par excellence. They have stressed that 'the earth is the Lord's and the fullness thereof' and accordingly that life here and now is to be enjoyed.

I believe that the modernists are right: Christianity must not be narrowed down to personal morality and evangelism. Its focus is not exclusively on a life hereafter and the professions do not fall into a hierarchy of spirituality. However, I also believe that although we are to be 'in the world' we are not to be 'of the world'. This is the criticism that the traditionalists have levelled at the modernists – of so capitulating to the world that they have lost the distinctive Christian message.

It is my conviction that the either/or, the traditionalists or the modernists, is an improper option. It is based on a misinformed perspective that splits life into two incompatible realms, sacred and the secular: either we withdraw from the world to the sacred realm with the traditionalists and become culturally irrelevant, or we capitulate to the world with the modernists and become spiritually impotent. What we need if we are to avoid the errors of either traditionalism or modernism is a Christian perspective that does not split life into sacred and secular realms. We need a perspective that integrates all areas of life as it is lived in this world under the one, spiritual, Lordship of Christ.

I am not alone in my concern that Christianity should be both culturally relevant *and* have a distinctive message. A number of organisations with the same concern have also recently emerged. This book is my contribution to the communal effort to make this a living reality.

The book divides into two parts. In the first part I

describe the split view of life that is pervasive in our society. I go on to explore the place of religious faith in life and show how, for better or worse, it moulds every other area of life. I then trace out a biblical faith that will mould a distinctively Christian way of life in all its aspects – both 'sacred' and 'secular'. In the second part I put this perspective to work by addressing several aspects of life in our modern world showing how these can be integrally Christian.

The main concern of this book is to bring all of life under the influence of the gospel. If this is to have any bite in our lives, then I believe, it must, from the beginning, focus its attention on our own lives as we live them now. For this reason I would like you to perform a small, but important, task before you read on. Take a piece of paper and draw on it a tree with seven branches. (See page xv.) Do not join the branches to the trunk. Down the trunk of the tree write a sentence which captures what you believe to be the heart of the gospel message. Then on each branch write the seven most important aspects of your lives: they may be your job, your friends, your family.... You may want to put twigs at the end of the branches to represent further subdivisions. Now think how you can join each of the branches to the trunk of the tree: how does the gospel as you understand it affect the different aspects of your life? Where you are sure that it does, join that particular branch to the trunk. Where you are not sure, draw a dotted line. If there is any area of life that you believe is unaffected by the gospel then leave that branch disconnected from the trunk of the tree.

At the end of the book we will return to this tree.

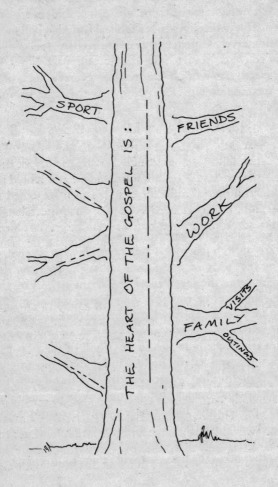

1
Sacred and Secular Splits

Keith is a Christian and a student at Cambridge University. He is keen on rowing and wants to join the university boat club. He casually raised the matter in one of the Christian fellowship meetings. During the prayer time, prayers were said for Keith intimating that it would be a wonderful opportunity for evangelism if he joined the boat club. Keith began to feel a little uncomfortable. He had to admit that evangelism was not his primary aim in joining the club. He simply liked rowing. He felt somewhat guilty and confused. Was he putting a worldly pleasure before service to the Lord? Was he beginning to 'backslide'?

John loved athletics. He spent all his spare moments training. Piles of athletics magazines lay round his house. He was also a committed Christian. Once when I visited him he told me that he had not been doing too well with the Lord lately. He had been spending too much time on his athletics and not enough time with God. Things changed, he said, when a converted Hindu came to stay with him. This man would rise every day at six a.m. and spend two hours in prayer and Bible study. John said that he was so challenged that he now spends much more time in prayer and reading the Bible and is back with God again.

John and the Christians in Keith's fellowship have done something that is common enough. They have mentally split up reality into two realms. The one realm of evangelism, personal piety and devotions is seen as the 'sacred' or 'spiritual' realm: it is the realm in which we are called by God to live and act. The other realm of rowing and athletics is seen as the 'worldly' or 'secular' realm. Christians, it is thought, should have as little as possible to do with this realm.

Other Christians make the sacred/secular split in different ways. They may set 'doing the Lord's work' over against 'doing ordinary jobs' for example. According to this view, if we really want to work 'full-time for the Lord' we will go to a Bible school and train to become a missionary or a pastor. Or if for some reason this is not open to us then we may choose to enter one of the 'slightly less spiritual' caring professions such as nursing. If we are well established in a 'secular' career such as engineering or commerce when we become Christians then we try to do the Lord's work after working hours. We join several church committees and involve ourselves in church work. Sometimes we hear of severe strains placed on family life because the husband and father is out so much doing the Lord's work. This highlights another associated sacred and secular splitting: this time between 'loving God' and 'loving people'. Devotional activities and church work are seen as loving God whilst enjoying husband, wife, family and friends is seen as an inferior human love. Yet in the Bible we find that loving people and loving God are inseparably bound (1 John 4.19–21).

At the heart of sacred-secular splitting, however, is the division made between the soul and the body. The soul is identified as that part of human nature that must be 'saved'. It is the object of our evangelism. It is the part of us that must be withdrawn from the world and the things of the body so that it may be nurtured in personal piety until at death it passes into eternal life. The splitting of the soul from the body underlays the argument in an article I once read on the theme of Christian rock music. The writer puts forward the case that rock music is anti-Christian and unspiritual because its focus is on 'rhythm', 'sensuality' and the 'body'.[1]

2

Splitting up life into sacred and secular compartments places us in an impossible dilemma. To be human is to be bodily and this bodiliness immerses us fully in the 'secular' world. We cannot escape our secularity, for to do so would be to escape our humanness. Indeed if we do try to escape we become estranged from God, from the world, from ourselves, and from each other.

We become estranged from God because we believe that God is not at all interested in the secular realm or, even worse, is hostile towards it. Yet we spend the majority of our time in ordinary 'secular' activities by virtue of our very humanness.

We become estranged from our world in that we withdraw from it. We interpret the biblical exhortation 'love not the world' to mean 'do not get involved in politics, art, rock music, etc.' Such non-involvement also results in impotence, and, having nothing to say to the needs of a culture, we become irrelevant. Ironically, in our very passivity we *are* implicitly loving the world in the wrong sense because our passivity implies that we are happy with the way things are.

We become estranged from ourselves and each other. A split view of life plays down or tries to avoid what it has identified as the lower nature. The emotions and the body become taboo. Emotional needs are then very often mis-identified as spiritual or moral problems. More prayer and devotional life or moral repentance are presented as the cure for many emotional ills including difficult relationships. Such counsel often increases a person's guilt and adds to the alienation that he or she already feels because it fails to meet the real need for genuine intimacy.

There are some strategies we can make to try and resolve our dilemma. The first is the 'balance' strategy: not too much 'secular' activity, just enough 'spiritual' activity; not too much athletics, just enough prayer and Bible reading; not too much church work, just enough time with friends and family; not too much time spent in evangelism but as much as possible without it adversely affecting other important activities in life.

However, this strategy is no real solution. It only covers over the inner tension and the problem remains. If we define 'spiritual' in terms of particular activities then whenever we do anything else we are being 'unspiritual'. Take the case of John the athlete. Because he has defined 'being close to God' in terms of prayer and Bible reading, then whenever he is doing his athletics (or indeed anything else) he is, by definition, 'not being close to God'.

A second strategy is to use every other dimension of life as a 'vehicle' for the 'spiritual'. If we are artists then all our paintings will have a religious theme. If we are musicians, we will use our music as an opportunity to preach the gospel. Some Christian performers have two sets of material: the one is their gospel set, the other is their secular set. If we are athletes we may be tempted to sew biblical texts on to our shorts! If we are engineers we will use our work place as a God-given opportunity to witness to Christ. If we are a Christian student then we will see the university campus as our mission field.

Again this strategy does little to resolve the dilemma. It simply bolsters the pervasive view that Christianity is a take-it-or-leave-it 'spiritual bit' added on to the other areas of life which are simply embraced uncritically. The Christian student's essay contains the same content as the non-Christian student's essay. The successful Christian musician simply emulates a secular lifestyle and values within a Christian sub-culture or else presents a message that the Christian life is about living with a foot in each of two different worlds.

The basic problem with all of these strategies is the misguided assumption that 'spiritual' means religious activities such as Bible reading, praying, confessing Christ and evangelism. The apostle Paul cannot possibly have understood spirituality to mean only these kinds of activities for this would make nonsense of such passages as Romans chapter 12 verse 1 in which he says: 'I urge you … to offer your bodies as living sacrifices, holy and pleasing to God – this is your *spiritual* act of worship.' 'Bodies' here means 'whole bodily existence' or simply 'self'. Paul's point is precisely that our whole lives – all our activities – must be spiritual.

We should not make the mistake, however, of thinking that it is only Christians who have a split view of life. The contemporary writer Ernest Becker in his prize-winning book *The Denial of Death* describes humans as split into two parts.

> Man is literally split in two: he has an awareness of his own splendid uniqueness in that he sticks out of nature with a towering majesty, and yet he goes back into the ground a few feet in order blindly and dumbly to rot and disappear forever. It is a terrifying dilemma to be in and to have to live with.[2]

Becker argues that it is the duality of our human nature that gives rise to culture. Our architecture, institutions, and art are, he argues, attempts to make ourselves immortal through the achievements that will outlive us. Through these we try to deny the fact that our very bodiliness means that we are doomed to die.

Only recently I was given a booklet on the theme of self-healing. The author bases his theory upon the premise that 'Our souls, which are really us, are immortal, and the bodies of which we are conscious are temporary, merely as horses we ride to go on a journey, or instruments we use to do a piece of work.'[3]

It is now a widely held view that the subordination of women to men that pervades our society is in part due to a splitting of the 'sacred soul' from the 'secular body'. The one is identified as the intellect and is thought to be a superior male endowment and the other is identified with the passions and sensuality and is thought to be an inferior female endowment.[4] Men then must subjugate lest they be tempted to 'lose their souls'. The writer Susan Griffin argues powerfully that even hard-core pornography is due to men projecting on to women their fear and despising of their own bodies.[5]

A split view of life is also intrinsic to the intellectual and scientific world view of our modern culture. When I first arrived in Cambridge I attended a course of seminars led by an eminent philosopher of science. Although there were only a dozen of us, she did not even once make eye contact with anyone in her class but lectured to the wall throughout the eight weeks. I was determined not to let her get away without some personal contact. After the last lecture when she had rushed out of the door and was already half way up the crowded stairs I managed to catch up with her. I touched her arm and thanked her for her stimulating lectures. Although she was obviously grateful, she also seemed quite alarmed. Cambridge University is archetypical in relating to people not as people but rather as 'minds on legs'.

The tone for our modern scientific intellectual culture was set by the philosopher René Descartes (1596–1650), who made a radical split between the intellect and the body. Only when we are completely objective can we obtain truth about the world, argued Descartes. We achieve this objectivity by 'lifting our minds out of our bodies'. Only thus do we purify our thought from all the subjective and misleading beliefs, opinions and sense impressions that we have picked up from the world around us. 'Objectivity' became the clarion call of modern science and yet another split was made between 'objective' science and 'subjective' religion. 'Have your subjective religious beliefs if you must,' says the scientist, 'but do not think that they have anything to do with truth. Science alone deals with matters of truth and falsity.' The modern philosopher A. J. Ayer speaks for many when he says:

> *The religious believer's* assertions cannot possibly be valid, but they cannot be invalid either. As he says nothing at all about the world, he cannot justly be accused of saying anything false, or anything for which he has insufficient grounds.[6]

Ayer does not even want to say that there is no God. He simply thinks that since we cannot settle the matter by scientific experiment it is meaningless to discuss whether God does or does not exist.

Descartes' splitting of the mind from the body also led our modern world into what the writer Karl Stern calls 'a fearful estrangement'. For Descartes the mind, or soul, is housed in a machine-like body embedded in a machine-like world. 'Just think', says Stern, 'of nature as nothing but a huge, vastly extended soulless machine which you can take apart experimentally and analyse mathematically, which you can run, but with which you have lost all oneness!'[7]

Stern argues that Descartes was driven to find refuge in his own intellect because he was not at all at home in his body, his feelings or with women. He was always complaining about being cold. In fact he made his famous intellectual discovery 'I think therefore I am' while he was 'sitting in a stove' trying to keep warm. His relationships with women were never satisfactory. He died of pneumonia while he was tutoring Queen Christina of Sweden in mathematics. She insisted on making her teacher rise at a cold, unearthly hour in the morning to begin her lessons. It is an interesting thought that our modern scientific world view might in part stem from the neurosis of one man!

We have seen that a split view of life is pervasive in the Christian and non-Christian world. In order to understand the phenomenon more fully we must ask the question where has it come from? The following quotation is the key.

> For the body is a source of endless trouble to us by reason of the mere requirement of food; and is liable also to diseases which overtake and impede us in the search after true being; it fills us full of loves, and lusts, and fears, and fancies of all kinds, and endless foolery, and in fact, as men say, takes away from us the power of thinking at all. Whence come wars, and fightings, and factions? whence but from the body and lusts of the body? Wars are occasioned by the love of money, and money has to be acquired for the sake and in the service of the body; and by reason of all these impediments we have no time to give to philosophy; and last and worst of all, even if we are at leisure and betake ourselves to some speculation the body is always breaking in upon us, causing turmoil and confusion in our inquiries and so amazing us that we are prevented from seeing the truth. It has been proved to us by experience that if we would have pure knowledge of anything we must be quit of the body – the soul in herself must behold all things in themselves; … I reckon we make the nearest approach to knowledge when we have the least possible intercourse or communion with the body, and are not surfeited with the bodily nature, but keep ourselves pure until the hour when God himself is pleased to release us and thus having got rid of the foolishness of the body we shall be pure and hold converse with the pure, and know of ourselves the clear light everywhere, which is no other than the light of truth.

This passage is taken from the writings of the ancient Greek philosopher Plato (5th–4th century BC).[8] Plato assumed that human nature consists of two incompatible elements – the pure immortal soul, identified as the intellect, and the impure body. Salvation, he believed, comes at death and with 'the release of the soul from the chains of the body'.[9]

It is in the writings of Plato, then, that we find the key to our modern views of human nature: the secular view which elevates the human intellect to a position of arbiter of all truth – indeed Aristotle after Plato called the human intellect 'divine' – and the 'Christian' view which sees salvation solely in terms of 'saving souls for heaven'. Plato saw the human task in terms of purifying the soul. We do this by resisting those things that pertain to the body and by devoting ourselves to intellectual meditation on the 'truth'. The 'Christianised' version of this is to purify our souls by avoiding the things of the 'flesh' and by devoting ourselves to the pursuit of personal piety. Plato would have probably been happy with the chorus we sometimes sing, 'And the things of earth grow strangely dim in the light of his glory and grace'.

Further evidence that Plato's views still run deep in Christianity is to be found in the way in which we have misunderstood the apostle Paul's use of the terms 'flesh' and 'spirit'. Paul used the terms not to denote a body/soul split but to denote a bodily life which is either influenced by the Spirit of God or by an idolatrous spirit. The New English Bible even wrongly translates 'flesh' and 'spirit' in Romans chapter 8 as 'Higher' and 'Lower' 'Natures'. As the biblical scholar Leander Keck says 'this is precisely what Paul does not mean.'[10] Indeed, the term 'soul' in the Bible is a poetic term that means 'self'. When Mary says 'My soul glorifies the Lord' (Luke 1.46) she means 'I, with my whole being, glorify the Lord'. When the psalmist says 'My soul finds rest in God alone' (Psalm 62.1) he means 'I, all of me, find rest in God alone'.

Plato indeed plays a crucial role in our modern split view of life but he did not invent it and this is important. A split view of life was already in the air that Plato breathed. He simply gave it philosophical articulation.

The New Testament theologian George Eldon Ladd argues in his book *The Pattern of New Testament Truth* that Plato was 'profoundly influenced' by the theology of the Orphic sect.[11] Since the sixth century BC, according to Ladd, this theology had been spreading throughout the Greek world and into Italy. The orphic theology is embodied in the following religious myth of Zagreus the bull.

Zagreus was the son of the great God Zeus. In a battle with the Titans, the wicked enemies of Zeus, Zagreus turned himself into a bull. The Titans tore him into shreds and ate him. Zeus in his anger sent a thunderbolt from heaven and struck the Titans. Out of the ashes rose the human race. Humans are therefore composed of a soul – the divine part from Zagreus and a body – the wicked part from the Titans.

In the last analysis the split view of life that is to be found in the thought of Plato and that is so pervasive and destructive in our lives goes back to a religious myth. We will examine the important implications of this in the next chapter.

2
Faith as Ultimate Concern

Religious myths are stories about the origin and meaning of life. They tell us the answers to our 'big questions', questions such as: Why are we here? Where does evil come from? What is our task in life? What happens to us when we die? The myth of Zagreus the bull, for example, tells us that we are here as a result of a cosmic battle among the gods. It tells us that evil is inherent in the bodily aspect of our human nature. It implies – the philosopher Plato later spelled this out – that we must struggle to free ourselves from our bodies until we die when the divine part of us, our souls, will return to their true home with the gods.

These answers to life's 'big questions' are embodied in stories simply because no other form of language is adequate. Certainly scientific language is inadequate. A religious myth is not a 'theory' about life. Its truth or falsity cannot be tested in a scientific sense. We cannot devise a scientific experiment in order to compare the nature of our world with that of other world's of whose origins we already have knowledge. We only have one world. We may be attracted to a particular myth for various reasons but in the last analysis we reject it or accept it by an act of faith.

Am I saying that all of us who have the split view of life I described in the last chapter subscribe by an act of faith to the myth of Zagreus the bull? Not quite. Obviously we do not all sit down with the myth story in front of us and then decide whether we are going to believe it or not. Rather, we absorb the answers the myth gives to life's big questions from the society in which we are born, through the way we are raised, our formal education and in a host of other ways. We breathe in these answers from the air around us.

We as individuals do not make a conscious faith commitment to the underlying myth of our society's world view because society in a sense does it for us. When we throw a stone into still water the ripples continue to move across the water long after the stone has sunk. Just so the ripples of a founding myth continue to move through human history long after the myth has been forgotten. In the case of Zagreus this ancient myth now long-forgotten has continued to mould a split way of looking at life for many generations of people. As long as our society continues to have this split view of life it is by its very acquiescence putting its faith in the original forming myth, even though this faith is now tacitly or unconsciously held. A striking example of how tacitly held faith works in a society and how the resulting 'world view' is passed on from generation to generation is to be found in a film made by the anthropologist Margaret Mead in 1959.[1] The film is about a day in the life of four families – Indian, French, Japanese and Canadian.

One part of the film is about babies' bath-time. In the Japanese family the mother gives the baby to the grandmother. The grandmother, who is seated in a large bathtub, holds the child close to her breast and scoops up the water onto him. Later the child plays with a very delicate toy owned and shared by all the children in the family, a lullaby is sung and he is put to bed in the family bedroom.

By contrast, in Canada, the mother places the baby in the bath on his own. A little tug of war game with the face flannel takes place between mother and child. Then the baby is methodically rubbed and scrubbed from top to toe. Later he plays with his own toy before being put to bed in his own bedroom. The light is put out and the

12

door is shut.

Two different kinds of values are expressed and passed on to the children in these two domestic scenes. In Japan: dependence, gentleness and selflessness; in Canada: independence, assertiveness and self-interest. Behind these values we can trace two different kinds of religious faith. In Japan, a combination of Buddhism, Shintoism and Confucianism gives rise to a belief in corporate identity of family and of nation. The individual maintains his or her identity by being a loyal member of the group. Harmony lies in selflessness and gentleness. Selfishness, independence and assertiveness are believed to destroy this harmony.

In Canada, Protestant Christianity coloured by Enlightenment humanism believes that God cares for the individual person, that the nature and destiny of humanity lies in the fulfilment of each autonomous individual, and that self-interest is the natural means by which this may happen.

If we were to ask the Japanese grandmother and the Canadian mother why they bath the baby in their particular way they would probably be unable to give reasons. They would perhaps appeal to common sense. Is this not the way it is done and always has been done? The values and the religious faith behind the values are tacitly or unconsciously held by the society to which they belong. These have, over the years, passed from focal awareness and have become incarnated in a way of life. Through this way of life they are passed on from generation to generation.

The film also illustrates well how religious faith – whether we are fully aware of that faith or not – powerfully directs the most ordinary activities of everyday life including the way we bring up our children.

The same religiously inspired impulses of loyalty, dependence and belonging can be seen in the modern Japanese company. Here workers and management are over against each other as rival power groups. The managers take care of the personal, social and religious needs of the workers in ways which are unheard of in our own country. Indeed the company appears to be more like an extended family than a business enterprise.

Again, the religiously inspired values of dependence, loyalty and belonging may be detected in the oriental family photograph where clothes and hairstyle are carefully chosen to comply with custom. Contrast a western family photograph where each member of the family chooses clothes and a hairstyle in order to express his or her individuality and independence.

Faith, then, plays a powerful formative role in human life but what exactly is faith? The great psychologist Sigmund Freud claimed that religious faith is, in reality, the projection of an emotional need. The young child feels safe when father is around and afraid when he is not. As the child grows older she begins to realise that the anxieties and fears in life that beset her are too great for even father to help ease. She then projects an all powerful substitute father figure 'into the sky'. In order to cope she must believe the illusion that God exists.

Other people have understood faith to be belief in, or intellectual assent to, certain doctrines, such as the Incarnation or the Trinity or the fall of humanity into sin or the verbal inspiration of the Bible. Faith, according to this view, is contrasted with scientific knowledge. Scientific knowledge, it is thought, gives us facts that cannot be doubted. Faith, on the other hand, requires an act of will because religious doctrines are not open to scientific proof.

There is, I believe, truth and error in both of these views. Freud was right to see the emotional element in faith – we will explore this later on in the book – but he was wrong to reduce faith to emotions. Again, belief in certain doctrines is an essential part of faith but faith cannot be reduced to beliefs. We will also return to this point later.

The psychologist Jung, Freud's former colleague who later became his rival, comes, I believe, nearer to the heart of faith. Jung turned Freud's view of faith upside down. He believed that faith is the impulse to have or to make something absolute or ideal: all-powerful; all-knowing; all-loving; all-wise. Faith, according to Jung, is not an adult version of a child's emotional need. Rather the child, in thinking her father absolute, is in fact exercising child-like faith.

It is the theologian Paul Tillich, however, who in my view comes even closer to the essence of faith. He describes faith as 'Ultimate Concern'. Our Ultimate Concern is that thing or person which we value most in life. It is 'Ultimate' because it is the very highest or deepest or most serious concern. It is 'Concern' because it preoccupies our thoughts, our time, our energy, our feelings. The psychologist of religion James Fowler lists some of the contenders for Ultimate Concern:

> … work, prestige and recognition, power and influence, wealth. One's ultimate concern may be invested in family, university, nation, or church. Love, sex and a loved partner might be the passionate centre of one's ultimate concern.[2]

Our Ultimate Concern is that thing, or person, or goal for which we would sacrifice all else. Paul Tillich writes:

> If a national group makes the life and growth of the nation its ultimate concern, it demands that all other concerns, economic well-being, health and life, family, aesthetic and cognitive truth, justice and humanity, be sacrificed.[3]

In order to see what your own Ultimate Concern might be you can do a little exercise. Reflect for a while on your life. Ask yourself what are the most important things to you in your life? What are the deepest desires of your heart; those things for which you would sacrifice all else? Perhaps your deepest desire is for a particular relationship or person, or maybe it is your career, or maybe it is your relationship with God. Try to be honest with yourself. Now take three small pieces of paper. Select three of the things that are most important to you. Write them on the pieces of paper. Set a wastepaper basket in front of you. Of which of these three most important things can you most easily let go? Tear up the piece of paper on which it is written and throw it away. Do the same with the second piece of paper. You are left with one piece of paper. On it is written the one thing in life that is most important to you, that which you simply cannot give up, the one thing that you would sacrifice everything else for and that you may even consider dying for. For you this one thing is non-negotiable. There is nothing which is more important to you. It is ultimate – your Ultimate Concern.

Faith understood as Ultimate Concern is to do with questions and answers about the meaning of life. The questions are not primarily intellectual or philosophical in nature; about the meaning of life in general, but 'what is the meaning of *my* life?' What am *I* doing here? Where am *I* going? What is *my* task in life? What will happen to *me* when I die?' The object of my Ultimate Concern provides answers for these kinds of question. If I were passionately in love for example, my beloved would be the meaning of my life. I would probably think that I was born to be with her, to share my life with her, that my task in life was simply to love her. In my romantic idealising I might think that I would be with her in heaven.

The answers I receive to my Ultimate Questions give my life direction and purpose. They give me something to live for. They give me identity – I know who I am and where I am going. And they give me certainty – I know the truth. All else is judged from the standpoint of the answers that I receive in faith.

Yet to receive these answers I need to play my part. Faith as Ultimate Concern involves action, probably the most important action humans can make. 'To have faith' is to give myself to, to trust myself to that which I believe will satisfy the deepest longings of my heart. Indeed, the extent to which I give myself over to an Ultimate Concern is the extent to which I receive answers to my Ultimate Questions. If I hold back, I become unsure of my identity and purpose in life.

Faith as Ultimate Concern also involves sacrifice and decision: to say yes to one Ultimate Concern is also to say no to another. Sometimes we get caught between two or more Ultimate Concerns. We cannot make up our minds which is really Ultimate. We are then thrown into confusion about our own identity and purpose in life.

Many people do not take responsibility for their own faith but simply 'go with the flow' of the faith perspective of the society to which they belong. But we can always expose a person's Ultimate Concern by asking 'why' questions of the kind that the child asks: Why are you at university? Because I want to improve my education. Why do you want to improve your education? Because then I will be able to get a good job. Why do you want a good job? Because then I will be able to have the things I want in life? Why do you want those things? Because.... When a person cannot give any more answers they have reached bedrock. They have come into contact with their faith, their Ultimate Concern that gives their lives meaning and direction.

Sometimes in life we are shocked out of complacency into taking stock of our lives and our Ultimate Concern. Recently I stayed at a monastery for a number of days. During a conversation with a novice I was told about the circumstances that had led him to take vows to become a monk. He had managed a night club in the West End of London. He woke up one morning and started to question seriously the life he was leading. He began to detest the materialistic values, not only of his immediate circle of friends, but also of the society to which he and they belonged. He wanted something more out of life, something deeper. His search finally led him to the monastery and to take vows of poverty and devotion to God and neighbour.

Often certain crisis points or stages in life force us to evaluate our Ultimate Concern; as a teenager when we are caught halfway between childhood and adulthood and are struggling to find our identity; or when we leave home for the first time and begin to get to know people who have very different beliefs to our own; or when middle-age arrives and we realise that we are not going to turn the world upside down in the way we thought we might; when a friend or member of our family dies; when illness hits us; when a love affair fails; or even when we are standing on a hill amongst mountains and feeling very small.

Not all of us after considering our Ultimate Concern end up by making such a dramatic change in life as the novice monk, and many of us, perhaps out of fear, find questions of Ultimate Concern too disturbing to ponder long. However, we cannot relieve ourselves of the responsibility of faith. A failure of nerve before life's Ultimate Questions means that we (in faith) settle for the answers that are embedded in our society and culture: material prosperity; career; fame, to name a few.

Faith as a universal human dimension of life cannot be reduced to any other dimension in life. Freud did not seem to recognise that our very ability to raise and receive answers to our Ultimate Questions speaks of a dimension of human nature which is more than just emotion. It is not a contradiction to say 'I am certain about the meaning and direction of my life but sometimes I do not feel certain.' If faith were the same as emotion this certainly would be a contradiction.

We should not reduce faith to emotion neither should we reduce it to belief in certain doctrines. At one time, 'to believe', which has the same derivation as 'to belove', meant 'to set one's heart on', a meaning which is indeed close to faith as Ultimate Concern.[4] But the word has changed so much under the impact of the 'intellectualisation' I described in the last chapter that its meaning has radically changed. Beliefs as we now have come to understand the word are intellectual articulations of faith. If I sat down and reflected theoretically on my 'Ultimate Concern' I could set down on paper my beliefs. These would help me to understand my faith more fully, but mere intellectual assent to these beliefs is not the heart of faith.

Faith cannot be reduced to emotions or beliefs yet it should not be sharply distinguished from knowledge. There is a ferment of debate taking place in this area amongst philosophers at the moment. It is not the purpose of this book to enter into this. Suffice it to say that many thinkers are now coming to see that not only is all knowledge, including scientific knowledge, founded upon faith but also that faith itself is a form of knowledge.[5] This conclusion is entirely consistent with the biblical understanding of faith: 'The fear of the Lord is the beginning of knowledge' (Prov. 1.7); 'By faith we understand that the universe was formed at God's command' (Heb. 11.3).

If we are to understand the nature of faith properly we should also see that the opposite of faith is not doubt. Doubt is in fact an important part of faith. Without doubt we do not grow in faith. We will consider this in more depth in a later chapter. The opposite of faith is 'nihilism' – the total inability to find any answers at all to life's 'big' questions. For the nihilist life is totally meaningless with no direction and purpose, no identity, no certainty.

Nihilism is an inhuman living death.

The force of this chapter has been that we all have faith. To have faith is essentially and unavoidably human because we all have our Ultimate Concern: we all raise and answer the great meaning questions of life. As an aspect of human nature faith is as natural as breathing, feeling and thinking. Atheists and agnostics, therefore, can no longer say to the Christian 'you have religious faith, I do not'. Rather the question is, in what or in whom does our faith lie? This is crucial because, as we have seen, our lives are moulded by our faith. When Paul Tillich wrote the words on nationalism I quoted above, he had Nazi Germany in mind. They alert us to the horrific consequences of misdirected faith.

Before we turn to consider true faith, I want to make one more point. The personal conversion of an individual from one Ultimate Concern to another takes place within and in terms of the 'world view' of the community to which he or she belongs. That is why a person may have a dramatic conversion to the Christian faith yet express his faith in terms of a split view of life that has its faith origins not in the Bible but in a pagan myth. The implication of this is that personal conversion is not enough. If we are to be thoroughly Christian in every area of our lives, if we are to have Christ as Lord of all of life, if we are to 'present our whole bodies as living sacrifices' to God, then our lives, in their entirety, must issue from biblical faith alone. It is to this that we must now turn our attention.

3
Christ – Our Ultimate Concern

... although they knew God, they neither glorified him as God nor gave thanks to him, but their thinking became futile and their foolish hearts were darkened. Although they claimed to be wise, they became fools and exchanged the glory of the immortal God for images made to look like mortal man and birds and animals and reptiles.... They exchanged the truth of God for a lie, and worshipped and served created things rather than the Creator – who is for ever praised (The apostle Paul, Romans 1.21–5).

The Bible is uncompromising. We have only two options when it comes to faith. Our faith, our Ultimate Concern, will be either our Creator – the true God revealed in Jesus Christ – or a creature, a false god, an idol.

We should not be misled by Paul's list of idols – birds, reptiles, etc. In his time idols were different from our own, but our idols are just as alive and well. I listed some of them in the last chapter. Neither should we be misled by the word 'worship'. In our secular climate, to talk of idol worship seems anachronistic. But, as we have already seen, everyone has faith whether they are conscious of it or not and faith leads to worship. As Paul implies in Romans 12.1,2, worship is an act in which our whole self is involved. It is the shape our lives take as they are moulded by a true or a false god.

If we choose to have the true God as our Ultimate

Concern, then, according to the Bible, we will have life in this world in all its fullness. If we choose to have a creature at the centre of our Ultimate Concern then we will have death, not just physical death, but a living death, closed down and cut off from the blessings of God (Deut. 30.16–19).

The Bible tells us that to surrender ourselves in faith to the true God is to surrender ourselves to the man in whom the fullness of the Deity lives (Col. 1.19). 'No-one', says Jesus Christ, 'comes to the Father except through me' (John 14.6). The historical Jesus, born in Bethlehem of Judaea, raised in Nazareth, crucified under Pontius Pilate, resurrected, alive and active today through the Holy Spirit, is the centre of Ultimate Concern for the Christian.

In Jesus our founding myth becomes historical fact. When we surrender ourselves to him we find distinctive answers to our searching, ultimate questions. We learn that Jesus is the one through whom we and all things were created:

> … by him all things were created: things in heaven and on earth, visible and invisible, whether thrones or powers or rulers or authorities; all things were created by him and for him (Col. 1.16).

We also learn that we, along with all humanity, became estranged or 'fell' away from God:

> There is no-one righteous, not even one;
>> there is no-one who understands,
>> no-one who seeks God.
> All have turned away,
>> they have together become worthless;
> there is no-one who does good,
>> not even one.

(Romans 3.10–12)

And we learn that through Christ God himself has rescued, or redeemed us from our fallen state and reconciled us to himself:

> For he has rescued us from the dominion of darkness and brought us into the kingdom of the Son he loves, in whom we have redemption, the forgiveness of sins.... For God was pleased to have his fullness dwell in him, and through him to reconcile to himself all things, whether things on earth or things in heaven, by making peace through his blood, shed on the cross (Col. 1.13–20).

These fundamental answers to our questions of Ultimate Concern are set out in the Bible in terms of a cosmic, mythological drama of the creation of the world, the fall of creation away from the Creator and the redemption of creation through Christ.[1] Before we go on to explore the implications of our founding Christian myth, it is essential that we understand the relationship between creation, fall and redemption, for this has often been misunderstood.

Firstly, redemption must be understood in the light of creation:

> In the beginning was the Word, and the Word was with God and the Word was God. He was with God in the beginning. Through him all things were made; without him nothing was made that has been made (John 1.1–3).

These opening verses in John's Gospel recapture the story of creation as it is dramatically told in the the opening verses of Genesis. They mean to tell us that the Word of God who became flesh in Jesus Christ for our redemption is the same Word through whom the world was

23

created. Indeed, it is *because* God is Creator that he is able to save us, as the prophet Isaiah knew well:

> This is what the Lord says –
>   your Redeemer, who formed you in the womb:
> I am the Lord,
> who made all things,
> who alone stretched out the heavens,
> who spread out the earth by myself ...
>
> Turn to me and be saved,
>   all you ends of the earth;
>   for I am God, and there is no other...
>
> (Isa. 44.24, 45.22)

The God who saves us is the God who made us. Although the Scriptures open with an account of creation, and although the New Testament reaffirms this teaching, many of us are so held in the grip of the split view of life we outlined in the first chapter that we only pay lip service to the biblical story of creation. As we have seen, more often than not, we think of salvation and the Christian life in terms of flight from the world rather than in terms of restoring *this* world to health and life. By so doing we force a wedge between creation and redemption. The apostle Paul, however, sees salvation in terms of creation redeemed:

> The creation waits in eager expectation for the sons of God to be revealed ... the creation itself will be liberated from its bondage to decay and brought into the glorious freedom of the children of God (Romans 8.19–21).

We do not, then, have a world which is fundamentally bad and therefore beyond redemption; we have a good creation which has fallen into bondage and awaits liberation.

Secondly, we must clearly separate the fall from creation. Christians who have a split view of life tend to collapse the one into the other. Instead of affirming an essentially good creation that has been corrupted by falling away from God, they effectively regard the world as intrinsically evil. Redemption is therefore impossible. The only option is to desert the world as though it were a sinking ship. Christianity then is reduced to a religion which is unconcerned with life in this world looking forward only to a world beyond this one.

Thirdly, although redemption must be understood in the light of creation, the two must not be conflated. This is a position that some modern theologians take up. Creation, or life itself as it unfolds in history, *is* redemption according to this view. Redemption is understood solely in terms of 'flowing with the process of life' and entails only that we continually change and grow. Although change and growth are important in life, as we shall see in a later chapter, according to this view there is no transcendent Creator to guide us on our journey. Humanity must, therefore, make its own rules and beliefs in life and change them when it is deemed necessary.[2]

Now that we have clarified the relationship between creation, fall and redemption we are ready to see how this threefold biblical theme informs our Christian perspective on life.

Creation

The creation story of the first chapter of Genesis takes us through the creation of material reality through vegetable, animal, and last of all human creatures, male and female. The repeated phrases 'Let there be' and 'according to their kinds', leave us with the impression not only of the sovereign power of the Creator over all aspects of his responsive creation, but also of the diversity and plurality of creation. Moreover, the repetition of the phrase 'And God saw that it was good' affirms the goodness of this diversity.

The diversity of created life is also manifested in individual creatures. Consider trees for example. We see that they grow; that they evoke different emotions and moods depending on their colouring and whether they have leaves in summer or are bare in winter; birds sit in their branches; their wood can be used for building houses. All this and much more makes up the tree. 'And God saw that it was good' (Gen. 1.12).

In human creatures too the diversity of life is manifested. We see that these creatures believe, feel, think, imagine, play, sing, dance, grow, create, are sexual and much more. 'And God saw that it was good.'

This picture of human nature is in striking contrast to the one we are presented with in the rival myth of Zagreus. There one part of human nature is understood as intrinsically evil. By interpreting the Bible under the influence of this myth some Christians have undervalued certain God-given dimensions of human nature. They have tended to assume that play, for example, is not as good or important as faith and personal morality. The Bible, however, is full of celebrations, songs, dances and festivals all ordained by God to express human playfulness (e.g. Exod. 15.20; Lev. 23.39–41; Luke 15.25–32). As the Christian philosopher Calvin Seerveld puts it: 'The Lord made room for a sense of humour, for fantasies of winged horses, for the fun of making-believe as when children "play house". And God saw that it was good.'[3] We may add that God also made room for feeling, thinking, growing and creating, and God saw that these too were good.

Relegating some aspects of our God-given human natures to an inferior position in creation is like saying that the goodness of trees lies in their use for building rather than in their beauty. The creation story gives us no directive to think of some aspects of creation or of our human natures as more valuable than others. It simply affirms that every created aspect that makes up our human nature is good.

One crucial dimension of human creatureliness, however, merits special attention. This is the task given by God to humanity of ruling over and subduing creation. In Genesis chapters 1 and 2, Adam, or 'earth person', is commissioned to work, or cultivate and take care of creation (1.28, 2.15). This call of God upon us cannot be avoided, for it is an essential aspect of our created human nature: for good or evil we *will* cultivate creation. The history of the human race is therefore a history of our response to this commission of God. Human culture, and I mean by culture every human activity not just the artistic and intellectual kind, is a history of human cultivation of creation. Governments; dinner parties; the clothes we wear; churches; pubs; football stadiums; atom bombs; are, for better or worse, all evidence of our response to God's call for us to cultivate and care for creation.

We can respond obediently or we can fall away from God's commission and therefore our humanness. We can create multi-national companies which are responsible to no one and that walk all over less privileged countries. We can set up schools that teach explicitly or implicitly that God is dead. We can pollute the land, sea, animals and our own bodies through economic greed. Men can make sure that they always grab the best in life at the expense of women. But we can never avoid responding to God's call for us to cultivate creation.

As one writer puts it:

In all our cultural activities and affairs – that is, in all human actions, artifacts, relationships and institutions by which we interact with and develop creation – human beings provide evidence of their God-given rule of the earth.[4]

A third important implication of the story of creation is that it is in this life that we find God. God walks with his human creatures in creation (Gen. 3.8). We do not withdraw from the world to an inner sanctuary in order to find God, as the Christian who holds a split view of life would have us believe. We have to do with God in every day life: the prophet Isaiah says that God is with us teaching us even the most mundane skills:

> When a farmer ploughs for planting, does he plough continually? Does he not sow caraway and scatter cummin? Does he not plant wheat in its place, barley in its plot, and spelt in its field? His God instructs him and teaches him the right way.
>
> Caraway is not threshed with a sledge, nor is a cartwheel rolled over cummin. Caraway is beaten out with a rod, and cummin with a stick. Grain must be ground to make bread; so one does not go on threshing it for ever. Though he drives the wheels of his threshing-cart over it, his horses do not grind it. All this comes from the Lord Almighty, wonderful in counsel and magnificent in wisdom (Isa. 28.24–9).

Many Christians retreat from the real world to the Bible. They live with the characters they find there as if they were in a 'hobbit' world. This is to misuse the Bible. The Bible sends us into the world we live in to look for God. The Wisdom writings in particular bid us to listen for the word of God in the press of everyday human social life:

> Does not wisdom call out?
> Does not understanding raise her voice?
> On the heights along the way,
>   where the paths meet, she takes her stand;
> beside the gates leading into the city,
>   at the entrances, she cries aloud.
>   (Prov. 8.1–3)

Indeed God may be found in the most unlikely places: in the political movements of a pagan ruler for example. With daring language the prophet Isaiah calls Cyrus of Persia God's 'anointed' (Isa. 45.1).

The implication of this is that we must never rule out anything or anyone from being a messenger of God. Indeed, the sayings of a non-Israelite king are recorded in Proverbs chapter 30, and what about Balaam's donkey (Num. 22.21ff)!? We should, then, always be listening for the voice of God, coming from Christian or non-Christian thinkers, writers, artists, politicians, etc.

We cannot, of course, indiscriminately accept everything we hear. 'Folly' as well as 'Wisdom' calls out from the world around us.

> She sits at the door of her house,
>   on a seat at the highest point of the city,
> calling to those who pass by,
>   who go straight on their way.
> 'Let all who are simple come in here!'
>   she says to those who lack judgment.
>
> (Prov. 9.14–16)

We are called to discern truth from error, God's voice from the 'lie of the devil'. How do we do this? Proverbs tells us: 'The fear of the Lord is the beginning of wisdom' (Prov. 9.10; see also Job 28.28). As we surrender ourselves in faith to God in Christ, and as our faith is nurtured by the Scriptures and in the community of faith, we begin to recognise more readily the voice of God. Thus we are more able to discern truth from error. Jesus says that 'his sheep follow him because they know his voice' (John 10.4). We tread carefully here though. There is little worse than a person who claims to know the voice of God. We should always remember that the truly wise person 'gives thought to his/her steps' (Prov. 14.15) and that:

> The wisdom from above is first pure, then peaceable, gentle, open to reason, full of mercy and good fruits, without uncertainty or insincerity (James 3.17, RSV).

God's presence is also to be discerned in inanimate life. The psalmists had only to look at a tree, or the snow and the rain and sense the presence of God calling it into being. We with our scientific view of the world see it as a self-explanatory closed system. We therefore tend to read the biblical account of creation as though it all happened a long time ago. We think that God started it all up and then disappeared to let nature run by its own 'natural' laws. But the Bible sees the creative Word of God as continuing to call creation into being, every second of every day.

We read in Psalm 147 verses 15–17:

> He sends his command to the earth;
> his word runs swiftly.
> He spreads the snow like wool
> and scatters the frost like ashes.
> He hurls down his hail like pebbles....

Can you imagine what it would be like to sense the presence of God around you in this way? The fact that we do not easily sense God's presence shows the formidable power of a world view or beliefs that are alien to Scripture. We look at trees and animals and we see them as belonging to an autonomous entity we call 'nature'. We do not see, or rather feel, that God is only a breath away every second, calling them to life. We do not hear them crying out the praises of God just by being there (see Psalm 148 below). We have to make a great effort to sense the presence of God in this world. But the people of the Old Testament Scriptures in everyday living sensed God all around them.

The biblical view of the world, however, does not make a mockery of the scientific enterprise. On the contrary, science is given a firm foundation precisely because God is faithful to his creation. He will continue to order and uphold it as he has promised.

Praise the Lord.

Praise the Lord from the heavens,
  Praise the Lord in the heights above.
Praise him, all his angels,
  praise him all his heavenly hosts.
Praise him, sun and moon,
  praise him, all you shining stars.
Praise him, you highest heavens
  and you waters above the skies.
Let them praise the name of the Lord,
  for he commanded and they were created.
He set them in place for ever and ever;
  he gave a decree that will never pass away.

(Ps. 148.1–6)

A split view of life wants to put God and the world into two incompatible realms. Take physical healing for example: if a sick person is healed through normal medical channels then we often call this 'natural' healing. But if a person is healed by the laying on of hands we say that God has healed him or her 'supernaturally'. The Bible, however, knows no such splitting up of reality into natural and supernatural realms. The apostle Paul, for example, experiences the comfort of God in the simple visit of his friend Titus: 'But God, who comforts the downcast, comforted us by the coming of Titus ...' (2 Cor. 7.6). I do not think that Paul for one moment believed that Titus was like a puppet in the hands of God.

He knew that Titus had made his own 'natural', free, decision and arrangements to visit him. He also knew that God's 'supernatural' hand was behind this visit – not one or the other but both at the same time. Similarly, the Bible would see all healing as both 'supernatural' and 'natural' whatever the means. As one theologian puts it:

'For Israel there was only one world of experience. The experiences of the world were for her always divine experiences as well, and the experiences of God were for her experiences of the world.'[5]

Fall

The story of creation tells us then that this good world is where we are called to be with God. We are to develop and care for creation in all its diversity listening out for God's voice and watching for his guiding hand.

The fall did not undermine any of this. After the fall, as we have seen, the psalmists continue to celebrate the goodness of creation and God's presence in it (see also Ps. 8). We shall see that God also continues to offer his guidance as we go about our cultivating task. What then does the story of the fall tell us?

Genesis chapter 3 tells us in mythological story form that essential to our human creatureliness is our freedom. Although we as creatures are totally dependent upon God for every aspect that makes up our lives we have the freedom to deny our dependence. The choice between accepting or rejecting our dependence upon God is presented in Genesis in terms of a cosmic drama in which two words 'hover above' us: the word of God and the word of the evil serpent. This is the picture of our human condition. We forever stand under these two words. It is important to recognise that both words are words of power for both God and the devil 'fight' for us and both words also offer us life (Gen. 2.9, 3.4). Only the word of God, however, is true to its promise; the other word leads to death.[6]

The phenomenon of pornography illustrates this last point well. The male temptation to pornography often begins with a genuine God-given need and call to intimacy. God calls us to walk one way in order to fulfil that need: by means of a loving committed relationship with another person. The evil one, the devil, calls us to walk another way: the way of impersonal pornography. Both 'words' promise life but the way of the devil ends in brokenness and alienation.[7]

When we reject God's gift of life we always put gods of our own making and imagining at the centre of our lives (see again the words of the apostle Paul at the beginning of this chapter). We then become dependent upon these substitute gods. Yet always they turn out to be cruel, life-denying tyrants. For the pornographer, sex becomes an idolatrous obsession. Eventually it undermines his sexual, moral, social and emotional integrity.

Idolatry is inseparable from another important biblical concept, the 'image of God'. In ancient religions, the statue of the god represented the presence and dominion of the god upon the earth. The statue or image reflected the character of the god. For example, the Philistines were a sea people. Their god had dominion over the sea. Its statue or image was fish-like. People who lived on land, on the other hand, were dependent upon the growth of their crops for food. They often worshipped fertility gods. The statues representing the gods would have oversized genitals. The Bible points out that in reality it is human creatures who will in fact image the gods they serve. 'Those who make them will be like them and so will all who trust in them,' says the psalmist with great insight (Ps. 115.8). If pornography becomes a man's god then he will begin to reflect in his lifestyle its dehumanising brutality in his attitudes towards women. Or if material prosperity becomes our idol we begin to value material possessions more than we do people.[8]

It is crucial we understand that although the fall does not undermine creation, nevertheless the fall pervades every dimension of creation. This is because we continually, and in every area of life, succumb to the lie of the devil. There is simply no area of life that is unaffected by sin, not our thinking, not our emotions, not our social relationships, not our art, not our faith. A split view of life not only limits creation, but it also limits sin – usually to areas of personal morality.

Redemption

The Scriptures tell us that despite our rebellion against him, God does not abandon us but continues to work for our redemption or rescue. Indeed this is the theme of the entire Bible. By setting out commandments and ordinances God immediately, yet again, offers fallen humanity the choice between the way of death and the way of life, the way of idolatry or his own way:

> See, I set before you today life and prosperity, death and destruction. For I command you today to love the Lord your God, to walk in his ways, and to keep his commands, decrees and laws; then you will live and increase, and the Lord your God will bless you in the land you are entering to possess.
> But if your heart turns away and you are not obedient, and if you are drawn away to bow down to other gods and worship them. I declare to you this day that you will certainly be destroyed ... I have set before you life and death, blessings and curses. Now choose life, so that you and your children may live. (Deut. 30.15–19).

Just as the fall is evident in every part of life, so is God's offer of life. The 'commands, decrees and laws' refer to the God-given plurality of human activities on this earth: Exodus 22.25 refers to economic life; Exodus 23.6 refers to justice; Deuteronomy 16.14 refers to festivity; Exodus 35 and 36 refers to artistic activity; Deuteronomy 8.7, 9 refers to technology; Deuteronomy 24.5 refers to personal relationships; Deuteronomy 23.13 refers to hygiene and so on. As we have already said, a split view of redemption narrows it down to only some areas of life: a Christian businessman pours vast amounts of money into evangelistic enterprises whilst making no attempt to redeem his unscrupulous business practice; a Christian musician preaches the gospel from stage but never stops to think redemptively about the culture she is part of.

We should not make the mistake however of thinking that the task of redemption is as simple as lifting out the above commandments and applying them in our time. This is what the Pharisees and Teachers of the Law of Jesus' time tried to do and met with scathing reprimand from Jesus. He accused them of laying burdens on people that were too heavy to bear. The apostle Paul refers to such practice as obeying the letter of the law while missing its spirit. He said this practice leads to death and is precisely what Jesus came to save us from. Indeed, we can recognise that redemption concerns all of life and then fall into a crushing legalism: God has a standard for us to meet (or rather fail to meet) wherever we turn and for whatever we do. Jesus, however, promised that on those who come to him he would place a yoke that is 'easy' and a burden that is 'light' (Matt. 11.30). The commandments of the Old Testament offered life to a particular generation and culture. In order to understand what it is to bring 'life' in our own times we must hearken to the words of Jesus and Paul that the spirit or meaning of the law is love: love of God and love of neighbour

(Matt. 22.37–40, Gal. 5.14). Of course the Old Testament is an essential guide to us but it must always be interpreted in the light of Christ who is both love incarnate and the centre of our faith.

The Christian task of redemption involves us in re-affirming the goodness of creation. This means that firstly, we must 'give space' to all the plurality of dimensions of life. We do not do this in a 'split' way of sanctifying certain areas, making them subservient to, and vehicles for other, 'more important' dimensions, but we affirm their goodness in their own right. Secondly, we must together nurture and grow in all areas, opening them up to life under the guidance of God. This involves continually freeing ourselves from the idolatry that has us clinging on to certain aspects of creation as though it were these that lead us into life. Only when we make Christ, the one who by his obedience to God is the perfect 'image of the invisible God', the centre of our Ultimate Concern is this a real possibility.[9]

4

... And God Made Room for the Self

I want to begin this section on putting our 'no-splits' theology to work by focusing on one of God's creatures that we seem to find great difficulty in giving space to: the self. A major reason for our difficulty is that many of us have adopted an erroneous theological belief that splits 'self' from 'others'. This belief states that we can only be concerned for the needs of others and be in a right relationship with a holy God when we are unconcerned about our own needs. Indeed, we often think that we have no right even to express our needs let alone have them met. This soon leads to a sense of worthlessness that pervades our self-perception or self-image.

It is my belief that God does not want us to have a poor self-image. On the contrary, he wants us to have a good self-image. Moreover, 'self' and 'others' should not be set over against each other for, as we shall see, only when we have a good sense of self will we be able to love others truly.

Before we discuss this further we will look at some of the factors that make up our self-image. The kind of self-image we have depends on such complex and various factors as sex, geographical and historical location, social position, the values of our local community, early parental bonding, images portrayed by popular culture, philosophical presuppositions and religious beliefs. For example, a daughter of an Aristotelian philosopher born over two thousand years ago in Greece would probably perceive herself as an inadequately formed male, inferior in every way to her male counterpart. (Perhaps you think that times have not changed that much!) Or a child who is repeatedly caused to feel shame by an over-anxious mother would be likely to have a poor adult self-image. She might be unhappy about her body. Indeed her very presence in the world might be a source of embarrassment. In our own time, popular culture has a strong input into self-image. Krystle Carrington and Bobby Ewing make us feel that our bodily lumps and bumps are in all the wrong places. Again, our self-image depends upon the values held by our immediate community. For example many students at university have a bad self-image because they are not as intellectually astute as other members of this institution which values us by our intellectual prowess. Or alternatively, we may live in a community which values technical or manual skills above all else, so we feel inadequate and embarrassed by our practical ineptitude.

Often our self-image is composed of contradictory elements which cause tension, confusion and frustration within ourselves as first the one image then the other vies for supremacy. For example, when a person is in church, she may *believe* that she is a child of God and therefore special, but when she is at work or at university, she falls under the influence of the twentieth-century humanistic world view, and begins to *think* of herself as a product of impersonal forces thrown up by mere chance. Or a person may *believe* that he is justified by faith, yet this life-changing belief may be frustrated from having its full effect by an underlying *feeling* of guilt, a feeling which has its roots in an emotional pattern established during infancy.

In this chapter I want to focus on two factors that play a particularly crucial role in determining the kind of image we have of ourselves. These are emotions and faith. First we will look at the emotional component of self-image.

God not only 'makes room' for emotions, he also calls us to grow and develop emotionally. We can recognise distinctive stages in emotional development just as we can recognise distinctive stages in physical development. The developmental stages of the first six years or so of life are particularly important, for the way in which we go through these stages influences the later image we have of ourselves.

The theological concept of the 'image of God' that we discussed in the last chapter is particularly important concerning the emotional development of children. Parents especially are called upon to play this mediating role. They are to 'image God' to their young children. The psychologist Jung appears to be getting at this when he said that children 'absolutise' their parents. (See Chapter 2, page 15.) Jung, however, did not work with the biblical idea of the 'image of God'; rather he implied that there is a 'necessary idolatry' involved in childhood. But God does not call parents to 'be God' to their children, he calls them to mediate his love to them.

However, we live in a fallen world and we are all imperfect. We do not perfectly image God in this world. Parents, to a greater or lesser degree, frustrate the call of God to their children. The result is that children do not hear the clear, unambiguous loving call of God to them.

Emotional development during the first six years of life appears to move through four recognisable stages. We may call these respectively: the newborn stage (up to about 3 months); early infancy (3 months to 1 year); toddlerhood (1 to 3 years); childhood (3 to 6 years).

God's word to a newborn child is: 'Let the child be at home, receive life, feel wanted and loved'. At the very worst, the child receives the message: 'you are not wanted or loved'. Some of us hear only this worst message, most of us hear a confusion of both messages. Even the most loving, devoted and caring mother often has to deal with her own powerful, negative emotions as her sometimes demanding child seems like a 'monster' to her.

The baby picks up the messages which are transmitted through the 'coldness' of the mother's body. If the more powerful message is negative, the child experiences rejection. He then begins to try to defend himself against the pain of rejection by 'freezing' his feelings. The freezing of feeling tends to appear in adult life as an 'escape into the head' and into abstract thought. Such people are likely to have a very poor body self-image and to feel inadequate in their personal relationships with others. They are fearful of intimacy.

The early infancy stage is the oral stage. It is marked by God's word to be nourished and to know that it is all right to need. Early deprivation may come about by a mother actually dying, or by her emotional withdrawal because of depression, for example. In which case the child hears the message: 'Your needs will not be met; you are bad to need'. This then leads to a self-image that is characterised by an inner feeling of emptiness and deep longing, clingingness to others and a sense of abandonment.

At the stage of toddlerhood, God calls the child to explore, experiment and to begin to 'stand on his own feet'. The conflicting message comes in the form of excessive and heavy-handed reprimand and shaming when explorations and adventures result in mishap. The self-image that develops is one of wanting not to be seen, extreme self-consciousness and embarrassment and is marked by an inability to step out and take initiative for fear of being shamed.

The childhood stage is the stage of sexual awareness. God's call is for the child to be affirmed in her sexuality. Since people in our modern society are quite sexually confused, she may well hear a conflicting message. The young sexually aware child crawls sensually on to her father's lap. If he is not comfortable with his own sexuality he 'freezes' or tenses his body against her. She senses that she is now not loved freely in the way she used to be. The message she hears is : 'Your sexuality is not good'. The underlying hurt pride gives rise to a tendency to stubbornness and also to an inability to love freely from the heart. It may also result in the splitting off of sex from love and even to promiscuity, for the underlying fear is, 'if I am sexual with the one I love then I will be rejected.'

Of course there is the opposite distortion of the sexual call of God at this stage. This is when the child is sexually abused. Our modern sexually confused society means that this also happens all too often.

Deep traumas then, experienced at different stages in our emotional development, will lead to various kinds of negative self-image. On the other hand 'good enough' parenting will provide the foundations for a positive self-image.

Faith also plays a leading role in the formation of self-image. As we have seen in an earlier chapter, by faith we receive answers to the 'big' questions in life, questions like: Who am I? What is my task in life? Where am I going? What is ultimately wrong in life? These answers provide an anchor for the self in the midst of all the other competing and sometimes contradictory images that demand our acceptance. If we have a weak faith, if we are not sure of who we are, what our task is, where we are going, and what is ultimately wrong in life, then we are like boats set adrift from their moorings. We are tossed to and fro between competing images in search of an identity.

But it is not only a weak faith that gives rise to a poor self-image. A strong faith may also do so if it is misdirected, i.e., if its content is not true to Scripture. Indeed, this seems to have been the case with the widely held Christian belief we talked about earlier – that only by denying our own needs can we meet the needs of others and be in a right relationship with a holy God.

The belief that lies behind the adoption of this negative self-image, i.e., that concern for self and concern for others are incompatible, needs to be examined in the light of the Bible. In particular, Matthew 22.39 and Luke 9.23–4 are pertinent texts.

In Matthew's Gospel Jesus, quoting from Leviticus (19.18) tells us that we must love our neighbours as we do ourselves. Whilst the focus of his words is on love for neighbour, they presuppose self-love. This presupposition rests on the assumption that there is complete solidarity within the human race. I am to love my neighbour because he or she is a member of the human race, created and loved by God. And I am to love myself because I too am a member of the human race created and loved by God. We do not have the human race on the one hand set over against myself on the other; we have the human race of which I am a part. The psychologist Erich Fromm writes:

> The idea expressed in the biblical 'Love thy neighbour as thyself!' implies that respect for one's own integrity and uniqueness, love for and understanding of one's own self, cannot be separated from respect and love and understanding for another individual. The love for my own self is inseparably connected with the love for any other being.[1]

In Luke's Gospel Jesus is recorded as saying: 'If anyone would come after me, he must deny himself and take up his cross daily and follow me.' At first sight, these words seem to imply that in order to be a Christian we must deny our own needs, and therefore they appear to contradict Jesus' words of Matthew 22.39. However, if we interpret the verse in the light of the focus of Scripture as a whole, i.e., on the call for us to have faith in the true God, we see that Jesus is not calling us to deny our needs, but to deny our idols. The tension lies not between love for God and love for self, but between worship of the true God and worship of self. (Idols are false gods of our making.) Jesus' words may be compared with the words of the Old Testament prophet Isaiah regarding cultic malpractices. Here the context of idolatry is clearer:

> But whoever sacrifices a bull
>   is like one who kills a man,
> and whoever offers a lamb,
>   like one who breaks a dog's neck;
> whoever makes a grain offering
>   is like one who presents pig's blood,
> and whoever burns memorial incense,
>   like one who worships an idol.
> They have chosen their own ways,
>   and their souls delight in their abominations.
>
> (Isa. 66.3)

It is helpful, then, to interpret the sayings of Jesus by making a distinction between self-worship and self-love. Whilst Jesus condemns self-worship, he affirms self-love. Indeed, experience shows that if we do not love self, i.e., recognise and meet our own needs, then we will not be able to obey the biblical command to love others. In order to understand this properly we should make a further distinction this time between selfishness and self-love.

Self-love recognises the difference between what may be termed the 'real' and the 'false' needs of the self. Selfishness, however, does not. For one person, self-love may mean recognising that an obsessive yearning to retreat from involvement in close relationships into a world of academic textbooks is in fact a false need. The real need is to feel wanted. For another, self-love understands that an overwhelming desire always to cling to others is a false need. The real need is to feel that her needs will be met. For yet another, self- love sees that always to shy away from taking the initiative is to feed a false need. The real need lies in wanting to feel supported and encouraged. For another, self-love sees that casual sexual relationships mask a real need to be lovingly affirmed as a sexual person.

Self-love then sees through the pretence of self-sufficiency and the games that we play in order to mask our own neediness. Selfish persons are unable to love themselves because they are unable to recognise their real needs. They are also unable to love others because they tie themselves up in 'useless rituals or in the search for illusionary fulfilment' as one writer puts it, and thus are constantly turned in upon themselves.[2]

Self-love is also opposed to self-worship for it knows that a saviour is needed. I have heard it said that to procure our own salvation is the ultimate in selfishness. This observation is quite wrong; to procure salvation is rather the ultimate expression of self-love and it is here that we also meet God's greatest desire for us.

Salvation from selfishness begins when we surrender ourselves into the arms of God. The story of Jesus told in Mark 10.13–16 is at the heart of the gospel. Jesus tells us that in order to enter the kingdom we must become like small children. Then he picks up the children and cuddles them. We enter the kingdom of God and the life and peace that characterises it by allowing ourselves to be picked up and cuddled by Jesus, no questions asked, no judgments made.

These verses have been (mis)understood too often in the light of Victorian sentimentality towards children. Many of us will have seen the pictures of rosy cheeked, blue-eyed little cherubs sitting around the immaculately groomed Jesus. But these obscure the profound message of the story. Theologians also often miss this important aspect of Jesus' work. They discuss all kinds of titles to try to capture the person and work of Christ: Christ the atoner for sin, Christ the revolutionary, Christ the Lord of life, etc., but they miss the crucial title of 'Jesus the cuddler'. In his parables Jesus tells us again and again what the kingdom is all about: it is like a woman searching and searching until she finds her lost coin; a father throwing his arms around a wayward son; a shepherd leaving the rest of the flock to rescue a lost sheep. The kingdom is about God's unconditional acceptance and love reaching out to us. Our task is simply to surrender ourselves into his arms.

If self-love bids us surrender to God's love, God's love is the foundation for self-love and love for others. Because we are loved by God who is the Creator of the world we know that we are worthy, that we are wanted, that our needs will be met, that we are affirmed in what we do and in our sexuality. And, because we are loved by God, we can be sure of our identity. We know who we are – loved children of God. We know what our task is in life – to help ourselves and others to find the life to which God calls us. We know where we are going – to life in all its fullness. We know what is wrong in life – brokenness and alienation from God, self and each other. Knowing our identity, we have a firm place on which to stand and from which we can offer support and help to others.

However, the transforming power of this foundational love can be, and in many cases is, frustrated by an inability to *feel* what we believe about ourselves: we may believe that we are loved and accepted but not feel it. We may believe that God will lovingly give us the desires of our hearts but not feel it. We may believe that God affirms us but not feel it. Unless we are able to feel that we are loved, our self-image will remain poor and we will not be able to love self or others. We will feel that we are unworthy of love, we will feel powerless and inadequate, and we will be unable to meet the needs of the poor and oppressed.

To sum up: love is indivisible. The degree to which I

am able to love myself is the degree to which I am able to love others. Selfishness and self-worship are the opposite of love, for they breathe death rather than life to self and to others. Love for self and others is founded upon the *belief* that we ourselves are loved by the Creator of the world, and upon the *feeling* that we are loved by the Creator of the world.

The implications of this, therefore, seem to be two-fold. Firstly, we need to look for a faith community which recognises that the core of the gospel is God's love and acceptance (of the whole person, not just a split off 'spiritual' part), and within which a positive self-image may be nurtured. This community may be found within the institutional church or it may be found outside (or alongside) the institutional church.

Secondly, we should seek to bring healing to our 'fallen' emotional selves. We do this by making space for our God-given emotions. I recently heard about a primary school where every class, teacher and child, began each day by sitting in a circle. Each person in turn was invited to express his or her feelings. One day they would talk about something that had made them happy. Another day they would talk about something that had made them cry (teacher too!). Yet another day one person would be singled out and the others would think of all the things that made him or her special. In this way all the children were affirmed and given space to speak and to be listened to. It is a wonderful way of opening up this part of life to God's call at an early age.[3] For those of us who are older, we may want to initiate a support group in which we can begin to explore in safety our early traumas and their affects on our adult lives. Or we may want to find a psychotherapist and engage in individual therapy.[4]

It is my belief that a positive self-image is both a result and a requirement of true Christian faith. While it is a gift of God, its attainment is also a human task. 'Work out your salvation with fear and trembling,' says the apostle

Paul, 'for it is God who works in you to will and to act according to his good purpose' (Phil. 2.12–13).

5
... And God Made Room for Style, Imagination and Play

If you live in the town where I do and you are suffering from such emotional stress that you are unable to cope with life, and if your GP is enlightened enough not to send you away with a prescription for anti-depressants, you may well be referred to the Health Authority's psychotherapy unit. After several weeks you will receive in the post a rather officious form offering you a consultation. The day arrives. You are still feeling distressed and you are now apprehensive about your appointment. You feel very vulnerable. You make your way to a side entrance in an oldish house. You enter a long corridor at the end of which is a 'patients this way' sign. You turn the corner and walk into a small waiting room.

In the waiting room there is a small table with some tatty and obscure magazines scattered on it. A row of unattractive chairs line one side of the room. On the walls are a few health authority posters. The room is lit by a strip light. To your left is a ribbed glass hatchway which joins the waiting room to the office. You peer through and wait for two women receptionists to finish their conversation. It goes on for some time but you lack the confidence to interrupt. At last, one of the women turns to you with an enquiring look. You explain that you have an appointment. The records are checked. You are told to take a seat. The women resume their conversation. You leaf through a few magazines. After a while a man appears wearing a white medical coat. His face is expressionless. He checks your name and asks you to follow him upstairs. You feel like crying.

When I think about what I have described I am angry. From the sign which informs you that you are a patient, the ribbed glass, the decor, the lighting; the attitude of the receptionists and consultant, you receive the message that you are uncared for. Just a little thought and imagination would have made all the difference. Maybe a few plants; some carefully chosen pictures; imaginative lighting; a welcoming and reassuring smile – you would have felt that someone cared. You might even have considered that God cares.

Now contrast the above with a dinner party I went to recently. The dinner table was set out with cutlery and tablemats carefully arranged. Two green candles spread soft, warm, light over the table. Green napkins, folded imaginatively, were placed in the wine glasses which caught and reflected the flickering candle light. The green of the napkins and candles were matched deliberately with leafy flowers placed in small vases, leafy vegetables for dips, and even the colour of the dips themselves. The whole sight made me feel joyful and cared for, and stirred up a small leap of worship and thanks to God.

What we are talking about in both of the above cases is 'style' and style is to do with the aesthetic dimension of life.[1] Style involves imagination and playfulness. Both of these are entailed in planning an aesthetically rich dinner party: setting out the table and choosing a colour theme. Both of these would also be involved if we had the authority to take aesthetic responsibility for the psychotherapy unit in the story above. We would experiment with furniture arrangements, decorating walls, hanging matching curtains; choosing soft directed lighting to cast playful shadows and to capture the intimacy that old-fashioned oil lamps once had.

God seems to delight in style. He instructed the tabernacle to be made in the most aesthetically indulgent way:

49

Make a curtain of blue, purple and scarlet yarn and finely twisted linen, with cherubim worked into it by a skilled craftsman. Hang it with gold hooks on four posts of acacia wood overlaid with gold and standing on four silver bases.... For the entrance to the tent make a curtain of blue, purple and scarlet yarn and finely twisted linen – the work of an embroiderer. Make gold hooks for this curtain and five posts of acacia wood overlaid with gold. And cast five bronze bases for them. (Exod. 26.31–7)

Jesus couched some of his most serious teaching about life and death, heaven and hell, in the aesthetic language of parables. Indeed the Bible, from Genesis through the Song of Songs to Revelation, brims over with aesthetic language, rich in symbol and metaphor. We have been so enslaved by the intellectualism I described in the first chapter that we have been dulled to the aesthetic richness of the language of the Bible. Consider the Gospels, for example. We analyse them into isolated verses and mine them for their intellectual propositions. In doing this we miss out on the movement, excitement, pathos and climax that is only to be found when we read the Gospels as a whole. Mark's Gospel, for example, tells the story of Jesus in terms of the gradual enlightenment of the disciples concerning Jesus' true identity. This reaches a climax with Peter's confession at Caesarea Philippi (Mark 8.27–30). Then the story takes a dramatic turn as Jesus begins to talk of his death. The pathos mounts and culminates in the crucifixion and burial of Jesus. The story takes another dramatic turn when the angel tells the two Marys and Salome that Jesus is risen. Most dramatic of all is the ending of the story (as it is in the most reliable manuscripts). The angel tells the women to go and tell the disciples the news. But 'trembling and bewildered, the women went out and fled from the tomb. They said nothing to anyone, because they were afraid' (Mark 16.8).

Luke also tells one of his resurrection stories with drama and pathos by employing a well-known literary device. He tells us of two despondent travellers on their way to Emmaus. They are joined by a third traveller the identity of whom is concealed from them, even as they engage in a lengthy conversation with him. However, at the outset of the story Luke lets us, the readers, into the secret that the third traveller is none other than Jesus himself (Luke 24.13–35).

Creation itself is in fact imbued with the playful and imaginative character of God. This is personified in Wisdom.

> The Lord brought me forth as the first of his works,
>   before his deeds of old;
> I was appointed from eternity,
>   from the beginning, before the world began
> ... when he marked out the foundations of the earth.
>   Then I was the craftsman at his side.
> I was filled with delight day after day,
>   rejoicing always in his presence,
> rejoicing in his whole world
>   and delighting in mankind.
>
> (Prov. 8.22, 29–31)

God delights in style then and style is part of the very fabric of creation. It is everywhere: in the clothes we wear; the houses in which we live; the way we walk, talk, laugh, the friends we have, the churches and pubs we go to, the offices we work in. God has ordered the world stylishly.

The aesthetic dimension of creation, moreover, exists in its own right. It cannot be reduced to any other dimension of life. Certainly style cannot be defined by a set of rules. This fact was brought home to me when I was in

Toronto in Canada. In that city a few attempts have been made to reproduce an English pub. Although the reproductions are ostensively accurate, I believe the attempts fail. Style cannot be reduced to a set of rules to be reproduced anywhere and at any time.

Like every other dimension of creation, God calls us to give space to the aesthetic dimension and to take responsibility for it. We are to nurture and develop it for God's glory and for love of self and neighbour. We cannot ignore it or pretend that it does not exist. The only alternative is that we walk in aesthetic disobedience. The affects of such disobedience are far-reaching. The above description of the psychotherapy unit illustrates this well.

Since the aesthetic dimension is planted everywhere by God, there are many ways in which we can walk with God in this part of creation. We can take time for seeing the man in the moon, and imagining clouds as 'curls and furls of angel hair'. We can watch raindrops trickle into rivulets down the window and guess which will reach the bottom first. We can experiment with colour schemes in the house, trying different paint finishes: playfully making wooden fire surrounds look like marble; painting a ceiling blue and mottling it with white so that it suggests clouds. As I have already said, there are no universal rules to follow, playful fantasy means that it is our imagination, our taste, our choice: God gives us that freedom.

We can be sensitive to style as we go about our everyday lives and our work. We can put flowers on our workdesk. We can be playful with the memos we send round the office. A Ph.D. student I know had to build a machine as part of his work. He could have made it purely functional but instead he made it stylishly. He even dressed it in balloons and streamers to celebrate its completion. If we have no aesthetic sensitivity as we go about our daily lives then we will become dull, cheerless people.

not simply 'naked apes' as the zoologist Desmond Morris would have us believe. We are human and aesthetically human at that. Our clothes are about much more than keeping the cold out. Aesthetically alive dress involves the fun of choosing clothes with style and colour that fit our personalities or the occasion.

Moreover, as with all other areas of life, the clothes we wear tell the world of the kind of God we worship. They may tell of a God who is imaginative and playful or they may tell of a God who is unconcerned with these areas of life. A university friend of mine was on the verge of becoming a Christian. She said sadly, 'I saw all the Christians out at their bookstall on the campus today. They looked so drab and nondescript in their dress that I do not feel that I can identify with them.' The drabness of the dress of many Christians may well betray a split view of life; a view of life which believes that God wishes us to concern ourselves only with an ethereal soul. Such a view will indeed pay little attention to style of dress. Yet we should be wary lest our clothes express a brokenness in ourselves. A person may be so insecure in her identity that she identifies herself with the latest archetype of fashion. Clothes, style and image then become an obsession. The stylish image defends the insecure self against the painful feeling of not counting. Such a perverted response to God's aesthetic call does not open up life to the blessings of joy, playfulness and abandonment promised to those who respond in aesthetic obedience, but closes down life. In the terms described in the previous chapter, what looks like too much love of self is actually not loving the self enough.

Now that we have seen some of the ways in which we can give space to the aesthetic dimension, and without leaving this theme completely behind, I want to focus on the play aspect of this dimension of creation. Discovery of the call to play can be a liberating experience. It certainly was for me. For many years now I have played the guitar in various bands. Before I was a Christian my entire identity was wrapped up in being a musician. Playing became an obsession. This led into a kind of masochism - being very 'down' on myself if no creativity was forthcoming. It was hardly a joyous celebration of God's aesthetic gift.

Then I became a Christian, and all this was turned upside down. I now saw my music solely as a vehicle for preaching the gospel. Most songs referred overtly to God and Jesus. They were all meant to persuade people to become Christians. I had now moved, as I came to see later, from the frying pan into the fire - from an idolatrous obsession with the aesthetic dimension to a sacrifice of all artistic integrity for the evangelistic cause. I measured the power of the Holy Spirit by how many people made a confession of faith after a concert. I no longer played 'secular' music in the pubs and clubs but played 'spiritual' music around the Christian concert circuit. As I became more and more immersed in a Christian 'subculture' I became more and more isolated from the world outside and, because I saw the message as the sole purpose for my art, I also began to value my music less and less.

Then, I really discovered God's aesthetic call (although I did not put it in these words at the time). This discovery came not so much as a call to a restoration of 'artistic integrity' but as a call to playfulness. It sent me back into the pubs and clubs to play rock and roll. The measure of the power of the Holy Spirit now became how much the band could lead its audience to a joyous, abandoned celebration of dance and fun. Gone was the obsession with artistic integrity. Gone was the obsession with preaching the gospel that by its very inappropriateness probably put more people off Christ than attracted them to him.

I am not saying here that evangelism of a direct nature is always wrong. What I am saying is, the reduction of faith to belief that we talked about in an earlier chapter has meant that we have also reduced evangelism to the imparting of information. We need to enlarge our concept of evangelism to mean a whole way of life. One aspect of evangelism as a way of life is an opened-up-to-God playfulness.

A split view of life makes play impossible. It robs God-given activity of its joyous life-giving power. In Chapter 1 of this book I introduced Keith, a Christian at Cambridge University who wanted to join the boat club simply because he enjoyed rowing. Fellow members of the Christian Union assumed that rowing is only legitimate if it is used for the purposes of direct evangelism. A split view of life sees God's gift of play as sinful indulgence or as frivolous because it sees it as belonging to the 'worldly' realm.

We may take the raw ingredients of play and 'cultivate' them in response to God's call of Genesis 2.15. For example, we may take the simple components of running, jumping and swerving and form them into a fully-fledged sport or game. We establish the best numbers of players and teams; we invent an appropriate pitch or board with boundaries to mark out the game from life outside; we construct special equipment; we invent terminology peculiar to the game; we train players in skills and techniques so that they can master the game. We establish goals and rules. And God sees that all of this is 'good'.

However, once we have done this in response to God's aesthetic call we may also infect sport with idolatry. As we have seen, idolatry means that all other dimensions of life are forced to serve the idol. Our idol may be physical fitness. Sport then becomes simply a means to that end. It may be economic gain. It may be character building. This is the old English public school idolatry from which I for one suffered. It led to the absurd situation where those who found no playful joy in rugger and cricket were held to the task with even more determination for, so it was believed, character building involves endurance. Our idol may be self-esteem. To win then is the aim of sport. As in the idolatry of clothing fashion, to find our identity in being a winner is to avoid facing and dealing with a more fundamental issue of self-image. The belief that sport is all about winning is also simply another manifestation of the general social idolatry of success through competition. Or, we may believe that sport is simply a means to the end of evangelism. I once heard of a Christian table tennis champion who was invited to play against an opponent at an evangelistic gathering. Afterwards he gave his testimony. The thinking behind this seems to be that the skill of this man would so impress the non-Christians present that they would also be impressed by his preaching. Also mixed up in this thinking seems to be the erroneous belief that Jesus will make you successful too.

It is important to clarify what I am and what I am not saying here. I am not saying that sport should not make us physically fit or build our characters or that there should be no competition or that God and Jesus should never be talked about on sporting occasions. Indeed, without the above ingredients, sport will be impoverished. Physical fitness, for example, takes a game to ever greater heights, and competition adds spice. I am saying that sport should not be understood as a means to one of these ends. God has made room for 'frolicsome fun' as one writer puts it and that as an end in itself should be the focus of sport in God's world.[2]

So far I have talked about the aesthetic dimension as it is embedded in all of life. Indeed, it is important that play, style and imagination are not to be seen as separate from the real business of life – as recreation that restores us for the serious 'unplayful' business of work. The concept of 'hobby' seems to imply this. No, we should be aesthetically alive and alert in whatever we do. Some of us, however, have a special calling in the area of aesthetics – to become artists. We can compare this call with the call that some of us have to deepen our thinking. All of us think things through, indeed, without this gift we would not last long in life, but some of us are called to be academics. Just so, all of us are called to express the aesthetic dimension of our lives while some of us are called to deepen this and become artists.

It is important to see that the gift and call to be an artist is as much a divine or 'spiritual' gift and call as it is to be a pastor, a missionary, or a nurse. In Exodus 35.30–3 we read:

> ... the Lord has chosen Bezalel ... and has filled him with the Spirit of God, with skill, ability, and knowledge in all kinds of crafts – to make artistic designs for work in gold, silver and bronze, to cut and set stones, to work in wood and to engage in all kinds of artistic craftsmanship.

In the case of theorising we have to learn certain skills in order to express our thoughts – we have to learn how to compare and contrast concepts, the rules of logic, writing, syntax, construction of argument, lecturing and so on. Similarly, the artist learns to finely tune her sensory awareness and to translate what she perceives on to a two dimensional canvas. She does this by means of colour, marks and shapes – a curve here to express movement, a jagged edge there to express anger and pain. The musician learns to play a musical instrument – a minor chord to express sorrow, a major chord to express joy, a ninth, eleventh note of the scale to express movement. And, when her artwork is complete we are invited to enter into its world. If we allow ourselves to be drawn in, our own imagination is fired so that we may see and feel something about life that we have never seen in quite that way before.

Earlier I said that there are no aesthetic universal rules. This does not mean that good and bad art is simply a matter of personal taste. Bad art, according to Calvin Seerveld, is to be identified as 'Kitsch'. Kitsch is imagination cheapened by sentimentality. It is a little Mexican boy with a teardrop rolling down the cheek, or it is sentimental choruses with simplistic melodies sung before the Eucharist. Kitsch 'thrives on sentimentality', 'it never enlarges our experience' because it never invites us to enter into anything new. 'Kitsch oversimplifies emotional nuances and reduces aesthetically sensitive life to one track, predictable, pseudo-transcendent satisfaction.'[3]

Art can also become ungodly by becoming idolatrous. In an earlier chapter we looked at what was effectively the idolatry of the human intellect. Now, instead of 'reason' being the arbiter of all truth, we have art. Art, not reason, the devotee tells us will take us right to the essence of life. Instead of an intellectual élite, this time we have an aesthetic élite. In hushed whispers we wander round the art gallery careful not to profane this sacred territory by letting on that we find the artist's work more opaque than leading us into all truth.

A friend of mine decided that she would play her part in redeeming art from élitism. She has rented a painting from a Christian artist, in the way that others rent their colour televisions and videos. The huge picture hangs on their living room wall for all to see. This move also helps provide an income for the struggling artist. Another friend has started putting plays on in a room at the village pub. All the actors are local people.

I want now to draw this chapter to a close by exploring the aesthetic dimension in relation to one institution that is close to the heart of most Christians – the Church. In particular Church liturgy. As a point of departure I want to use an article I have in front of me. It is written by Dr

Peter Masters and is called 'How Images Destroy Faith'.[4] In the article Dr Masters argues that any 'visual representation' of God, 'choirs singing complex and sophisticated musical arrangements' and the like are not only detrimental to true worship but are explicitly forbidden by God in the commandment forbidding idolatry. He asks 'How would we represent sublime holiness and justice? Can we make anything which is totally flawless and stunningly perfect? Can we depict unfathomable mercy and love? ... Only by the words which God has chosen can we gain a right impression of our great and glorious heavenly king.'

Now it is true that in church the aesthetic dimension of liturgy can turn into an idolatry. Occasionally, I attend evensong in King's College chapel in Cambridge and when I see all the tourists in the congregation I wonder if some of them are there for worship of the liturgy rather than for worship of God. However, this is a very different matter to saying that the presence of images, symbols and skilfully sung songs is necessarily idolatry. To make this jump is to banish the aesthetic dimension to the realms of sinfulness. In fact Dr Masters betrays his own (idolatrous?) bias in his argument – a bias in favour of abstract concepts and therefore intellectualism. Moreover, the abstract concepts he prefers to use to refer to God: 'sublime', 'totally flawless', 'stunningly perfect' are not to be found in the Bible. There we find concrete imagery such as 'shepherd', 'rock', 'king'. The fact is we can never drain imagery and symbol from our liturgy. Why? Because God has planted the aesthetic dimension at the heart of creation and this includes liturgy. Indeed, liturgy and worship are founded upon the aesthetic dimension of life. Every action we do in church symbolises what we believe about God. We kneel to pray and it tells that God is to be approached with honour and humility. We sit to pray and it tells that God comes to us just as we are. We go forward for communion and it tells that God beckons us to him. We remain in our seats while the bread and wine is brought to us. This tells that God takes the initiative in coming to us. I wonder sometimes why dance in church often seems to have an ethereal quality to it – a wafting around like angels. Does this not betray a belief that God is opposed to the body?

Even the style of our buildings tells something of the God we worship. A tin hut says that God is close to us in our everyday life. A cathedral with towering spires and buttresses tells of a God who is majestic, transcendent and the Lord of the universe.

No, God does not want us to try to suppress the aesthetic dimension with its expression in symbols and images, for it is precisely through these that we encounter him. Rather, he calls us to take responsibility for them, to fashion and form them so that they tell the world who our God is.

We may wish to leave our images and symbols 'as simple as possible' as Dr Masters prefers. We should not be fooled into thinking, however, that we have done away with them altogether as when he says, 'All man-made models and figures must go, and then the shutters of Heaven will roll aside, and we shall be able to perceive the glory and greatness of our heavenly Father.' Our unformed symbols will testify just as powerfully to who it is we worship as do our sophisticated symbols. We should take care lest our liturgy, like the clothes we wear, speaks of a god who is anti-life rather than of a God who is for life in all its fullness:

> May the glory of the Lord endure for ever;
> > may the Lord rejoice in his works –
> he who looks at the earth, and it trembles,
> > who touches the mountains, and they smoke.
> I will sing to the Lord all my life;
> > I will sing praise to my God as long as I live.
>
> (Ps. 104.31–3)

6

... And God Made Room for Faith Development

The film *Francis* is the tragic story of the Hollywood actress Francis Farmer. At one point in the film Francis tells us of the beginning of her atheism. At the age of six years, after she had had her bath, she would lie naked on her bed and experience the presence of God as she lay there feeling clean and pure. One Sunday, her Sunday school teacher explained to the children that God must be understood as a Trinity – Father, Son and Holy Ghost. Francis was bitterly disappointed for she now knew that her bathtime experience was not an experience of God at all. This story is very sad because it tells of a mistake. The image that Francis had of God was not the same image that her minister had but it was no more wrong than his. She and her minister were simply at different stages in their faith development. It is faith development that I want to look at in this chapter.

James Fowler, an American psychologist of religion, in his important and original book *Stages of Faith* has traced out recognisable stages in the development of human faith and our images of God. Fowler's work forms the basis of this chapter.[1]

If we have a split view of life we may well find the idea of human faith development difficult to accept. There are two main reasons for this. The first is that development implies change and a split view of life tends to distrust change. The lingering influence of Platonic philosophical ideas is largely responsible for this. Plato linked change with imperfection and changelessness with perfection. His concept of God therefore was of a being who did not change. But we need to make a distinction between God and our images of God. It is through our finite and human images that God comes to us and that we experience him. We all experience and relate to God in terms of images drawn from the world around us. The Bible helps us with this by guiding us in our imaging. There, God is presented to us as rock, shepherd, king, shield, father, judge, etc.

These images, moreover, are not static but are vibrantly alive. They are infused with moral, emotional and imaginative content. We are conscious of our moral responsibility when we think of God as judge. We feel supported by God as rock. We imagine him as a shepherd carrying us close to his breast. As we grow and develop morally, emotionally, imaginatively, and intellectually so our images of God and indeed our ways of relating to God change and develop. Indeed, if our images of God do not change this is a sure indication that we are not growing in these areas and since they are foundational to our faith it is also a sure indication that we are not growing in faith either.

Secondly, a Christian split view of life wants to understand faith as a unique gift to Christians and as a supernatural revelation of God's nature. In one sense this is true, in another sense it is not true. In order to understand this it is helpful to make a distinction between the form of our faith and the content of our faith. I have already shown in an earlier chapter that faith is a divine gift to all humanity, not only to Christians. God calls all his human creatures to nurture and develop their faith as surely as he calls them to develop physically and emotionally. This universal gift of faith is the form of faith. However, the content of our faith, i.e., our images of God or of whatever we take to be Ultimate (see Chapter 2), differs radically depending on our religious orientation. Hindus,

Marxists and Buddhists will have different content to their faith even though the form will exhibit similar characteristics if each person is at the same stage of faith. If the content of our faith is focused on Jesus Christ, then we affirm that this is indeed a special gift of the Holy Spirit.

We will now turn to the stages of faith themselves, paying particular attention to the dangers involved in faith development through each stage and in moving from one stage to another.

From the time of our birth we are thoroughly human. We have not of course developed all our human faculties but they are all present waiting to be unfolded in the fullness of time. This is no less true for faith. The faith of a baby is not like adult faith. It is not differentiated out from his or her total experience. As we saw in an earlier chapter, the child is not at the stage of life where he or she can understand that the world, God and mother are separate from each other. The faith of a baby is particularly fused with sensual experience. As we have also seen in an earlier chapter, through bodily contact with the mother the child receives either the message that she is loved and wanted or the message that she is unloved and unwanted. Thus at this very early stage the foundation for our images of God and way of relating to God is laid, of trust or mistrust, acceptance or rejection.

As a child grows she begins to develop her capacity to use language and imagination. This is as yet unrestrained by logical thought which has not fully developed. Her imagination is therefore able to 'run riot'. Fairies, goblins, giants, monsters, and Father Christmas all inhabit the child's world. Through these kinds of images the child is able to express her primitive emotions – fear, anxiety, love, etc. – and through these images she relates to God. Parents and others who play an important part in the life of the child may feed her imagination with stories of love, loyalty, bravery and other life-giving images or they may exploit the child's vivid imagination by using it to control her. Confronting a child with phrases like, 'If you do not behave then the bogey men will come after you', or perhaps worse ' … God will get his stick out to you', will give rise to fear and anxiety in the child. Another danger is the one we have already seen concerning Francis Farmer: parents and others may dismiss the child's images and ways of relating to God as false. I once heard a theological student address the children in church. He was trying to explain to them the meaning of the story of Adam and Eve by drawing out three propositions about our relationship with God. By the looks on the children's faces it was obvious he was leaving them cold. No wonder! Genesis as a story speaks to the child in the language that he knows. Children are not able to relate to intellectual abstractions at this stage in their lives.

From about the age of eight years, the child's intellectual faculty develops rapidly and he is more able to sort out fantasy from fact – Father Christmas and fairies are not real whereas God is real. The 'ultimate horizon' of life, still pictured in terms of vivid images, settles down and is experienced in terms of more orderly and meaningful stories. God at this stage is pictured in very human terms – as a robed figure with white beard and hair, for example.

The orderliness of the world is also accompanied by a sense of lawfulness, balance and reciprocity concerning God and his dealings with us. Fowler interviews a Roman Catholic woman who shows clear evidence of this stage of faith. (This interview also illustrates how a person may get 'stuck' at an immature level of faith.) She believes and teaches her children that they should build up a 'bank account' of prayers so that when they are in trouble they can draw on this 'capital' for help.[2]

As a child enters her teens and her intellect develops further she is able to take theoretical distance not only from former faith stories, but also from herself. She becomes acutely aware of her appearance to others. Young teenagers try several devices in order to hide their self-embarrassment. I am picturing now the kids at our local fish and chip shop hanging around the video machine; they are smoking, chewing gum, looking nonchalant and also very self-conscious!

This is the stage of friendship and young love. For the first time the child forms a close relationship with someone outside the family. The two friends become close pals, sharing interests, their lives and dreams. Through this intimate relationship the greater depths of human personality are discovered and correspondingly the young teenager's image of God is also deepened. God is now understood as caring and supportive. This image can have a much needed stabilising effect: this stage in life is often marked by identity confusion or even crisis as the young person is caught between childhood and adulthood and between different, sometimes conflicting authorities – family, school, church.

This stage may also be marked by a leaning on external authority. It may be a church fellowship or a religious group. It may also involve charismatic leaders whose teaching and perspective on life is taken on and is largely unquestioned. Orthodoxy is often identified with the theology of one's own community. The boundaries are quite rigidly drawn. One is either in or out.

Fowler believes that many people do not move on from this stage of faith to the next which is entered through critically examining one's own faith and is appropriate in late teens or early twenties. Indeed, many Christian churches and groups seem to want to stop people from moving on by discouraging radical questioning. Some extreme forms of 'shepherding', for example, overtly discourage questioning of the central doctrines of their community. I know someone whose searching questions led to his excommunication on the grounds that he was a subversive. So severe was this excommunication that the rest of the church were warned that if they continued to associate with him they too would be cut off from the community and by implication from God's favour too. In other churches the message to conform is less overt. It is implicit in the preaching, teaching and language of the community and the assumption that its own theological perspective is to be equated with the truth and that this is beyond criticism or questioning.

The taboo placed on critical questioning is also inherent in the wider Christian community. I once reviewed a book on the subject of Christian marriage written by a couple who were renowned leaders of a particular wing of the Christian church. The book promised to be of help to those who were finding marriage a struggle. At the outset the book boasted a complete openness. However, it did not take long to realise that the openness was in fact well-bounded. Certain relationship problems of a comparatively minor nature were indeed aired freely as were their successful solution. However, any married couple who were experiencing more severe marital problems and who needed to deal with more radical questions would feel that this community was not the place where they could do this. The book in effect was a covert set of rules of behaviour for acceptable community (meaning Christian community!) membership.

A faith community which exploits a person's faith and refuses to let her faith life develop is obviously dangerous. It can also lead to much bitterness. When we allow someone we admire to do our thinking for us or to tell us what we can and cannot believe, we give part of our own 'soul' to them. After a while when we realise what we have done we inevitably feel resentful. It is nearly always true that sooner or later when a person realises what has happened their admiration turns into resentment.

The transition to the next stage of faith is brought on

by the need to further establish our own individual identity apart from any one group. God calls us at this stage to make our faith our own. If the transition occurs at all it is often brought on by the experience of moving away from home and away from our former faith community.

In particular, many people who go off to university soon find themselves calling many of their earlier beliefs into question. The transition to this stage of faith is often a time of great crisis. For a time some people find that the rug is being pulled out from under their feet as the beliefs and values that have sustained them throughout their life are challenged: a psychology lecturer argues powerfully that belief in God is an illusory, emotional need for a parent figure; a Marxist sociologist tries to persuade us that religious beliefs are moulded completely by political factors; a theology lecturer tells us that most of Jesus' words recorded in the Gospels were put onto his lips by the early church.

Some Christians respond to the challenge of secular ideas by giving up their faith in order to preserve their intellectual integrity. Fowler captures well this kind of response by referring to an experience of the theologian Harvey Cox. Harvey Cox, himself a Baptist, would sometimes go to a Catholic church with his friends. At one period of time he was going out with a Catholic girl who, being older than he, went off to college to study anthropology. She returned home for the Christmas holidays and together on Christmas Eve they went to a beautiful midnight Mass. At the high point of the Mass, as the people were receiving the Eucharist, Harvey Cox's girlfriend whispered in his ear:

> That's just a primitive totemic ritual you know.... Almost all premodern religious and tribal groups have them. They are ceremonies where worshippers bind themselves together and to the power of the sacred by a cannibalistic act of ingesting the mana of a dead god'.

Communion, Cox said, was never the same again.[3]

Other Christians lead a 'schizophrenic' life. They keep at bay any impending crisis to their faith by putting their faith and their studies into two water-tight compartments. They become two people: in their essays they write what they do not believe. In the Christian fellowship they confess what they dare not write in their essays. By refusing to face the issues these Christians also do not grow to maturity in their faith.

Thankfully, a third group of Christians is beginning to emerge. These Christians are taking seriously both their faith and secular ideas. They are wanting to bring their Christian faith to bear critically on secular theories as well as examine their former faith images in the light of well-tested secular ideas. Much of my work with College House in Cambridge is with Christian students such as these.

The danger that lurks with this stage of faith is an exaggerated confidence that the human intellect and critical thought will lead us into all truth. Former meaningful images and stories that sustained us may well be lost for ever, replaced by unimaginative and sterile intellectual concepts. Moreover, given the idolatry of the human intellect that is rife in our society, people at this stage of faith often fall into the trap of enforcing it as the norm on all of us. We have already seen evidence of this with Francis Farmer and with the theological student's children's address.

Fowler believes that the next stage of faith is rarely entered before mid-life if at all. The transition comes about when earlier meaningful faith images insist on re-asserting themselves to challenge the neat intellectual faith scheme that we constructed at the intellectual stage. It believes that the intellectual stage may have been guilty of 'murdering' early faith images and stories through critical dissection. A person at this new stage of faith is more ready to humble himself or herself before stories and images held earlier. She lets these rather than her intellect do the judging in matters of ultimate truth. The stage develops into a calm confidence and trust in its own faith perspective, stories and images. This calm confidence means that it is not threatened by other faith perspectives; rather it gives rise to an openness to other perspectives and a willingness to learn and grow.

This stage of faith is often entered through a passage of great emotional upheaval and distress of the kind that many experience when entering mid-life. A person begins to face the fact that they must 'let be' and 'let go'. They must acknowledge and let be their own ageing, they must let go of their disappearing youth and unfulfilled hopes and dreams. They must let go of the intellectual conceit that was theirs in the earlier faith stage. In the process of letting go and letting be they become aware of the deeper aspects of the human psyche, of their own and of others. They recognise that unconscious feelings, needs and beliefs mould our conscious beliefs. Because they recognise this they develop a non-judgmental attitude towards others. It is not the case, as it might seem, that this stage is a return to a pre-critical stage of faith. Rather, the intellect is dethroned from its lofty position as arbiter of all truth and is integrated with other important dimensions of the self, such as emotions and imagination.

The danger of this stage of faith lies in its very tolerance and openness. For close behind these is the temptation to complacency. Letting go of some of one's own strongly held convictions can easily turn into a complacency towards the ideas and actions of others whether or not we agree with them. The desire and motivation to change things in the world then ebbs away.

Before we go on to see what we can learn from this analysis of faith stages, some general observations should be made. Firstly, movement from one stage of faith to another does not necessarily mean conversion although it may do. Conversion is more to do with the content of faith images and stories. Someone may be converted from Buddhism to Christianity in their twenties, for example, and still exhibit the same critical form of faith.

Secondly, the question of which is the true or right stage of faith can only be considered in the context of age. Appropriateness is a better term. It is inappropriate, therefore, for a thirty-year-old to have the faith of a teenager. Some people stay stuck at one stage of faith in which case we would call their faith underdeveloped or immature.

Thirdly, a faith community may exhibit the characteristics of a relatively mature stage of faith yet individuals within it may be at an earlier stage of faith. For example, a particular Christian fellowship may be very critical and intellectual about its faith. A teenager who belongs to this fellowship may also express himself in the same way. However, he may not yet have made this faith his own. He has uncritically accepted the intellectual style and teaching of his leaders.

Fourthly, you may have been able to recognise some aspects of all five stages in your own faith. This points to the fact that the movement from one stage to the other is not so much a linear progression but more like a change in focus. All other stages of faith are present to greater or lesser degree in all of us.

I believe that the concept of faith stages is illuminating and helpful. In conclusion I want to list some of the things that it teaches us. We can learn that change and development is a good part of God's creation. We should not distrust change and think that it is bad but rather help people to change in a way that is pleasing to God.

As a church we can help individual members more effectively in their pilgrimage of faith. We no longer must expect a child to have the same images of God as an adult. We now recognise that the critical questioning of a nineteen-year-old student does not necessarily signify the death of his faith but we see that God is calling him to make his faith his own. Indeed, we make room for radical questions. If a person's questioning heart means that she has to leave her church, then the church has failed her. Neither should the church be quick to condemn the middle-aged Christian as a complacent 'liberal' but rather trust and appreciate her hard won tolerance and wisdom. More generally, when we perceive that a person has been stuck too long at one particular faith stage, we should encourage him to continue his faith journey supporting him through the often painful process of transition to another faith stage.

7

... And God Made Room for Justice

When people use the word 'justice' they usually assume that we all know what is meant. In fact how we understand justice depends upon certain beliefs we have about life. If we believe or accept that slavery is right, for example, then we will think that it is 'just' to punish a runaway slave. If we believe that animals are more like machines than like humans then we will think that it is not at all unjust to stack up chickens in batteries one upon the other so that they cannot move. With clear consciences we will place them in artificial light so that they lay eggs more intensively during their shortened life.

These beliefs we have about life are, moreover, like our ideas about bathing babies (see Chapter 2), moulded by religious faith. The belief that animals are more like machines than like humans for example, stems again from a split view of human nature – that we are minds housed in machine-like bodies shared with the animals. This split view of human nature was articulated by the philosopher Descartes and has its origins in the religious myth of Zagreus the bull that we described in Chapter 1.

We can see more easily the faith origin of other ideas about justice. For example, if we believe that God is male and that humans are made in the image of God then we will think it 'just' for men to rule over women. If we believe that homosexuality is sinful then we may well think it 'just' to pass a law forbidding the promotion of a homosexual lifestyle. If we believe that religion was invented by the powerful in order to divert the powerless from thinking about their condition then we will think it 'just' to outlaw missions and evangelism.

It is clear, then, that in the last analysis what we believe about justice and how we carry out justice is, like all other areas of life, dependent upon faith. If we are to gain a Christian understanding we need, therefore, to turn to the Bible to shed light on the meaning of justice. But before we do this we must deal with a major problem that many Christians have in this area.

This problem concerns the relationship between the Bible and politics. As we shall see later, politics is to do with the administration of justice. It is the task of rulers, governments, kings, etc. There is currently an erroneous and pervasive belief that the Bible has no political content. This belief again arises from a split view of life. By equating the spiritual with 'other-worldly' we become blind to the 'this-worldly' political content of the Bible. I do not think that I have come across anything more ironic than the comment made unwittingly by a Christian that there was no political content in the biblical books of Kings and Judges. His blindness was so great that he was even unable to take the hint from the titles of the books! There is in fact so much political content in the Bible that it is difficult to know where to start. We read again and again that God is just (see for example Deut. 32.4, Ps. 89.14 and 96.13, Isa. 51.4ff) and that he is concerned that there be justice upon the earth. In fact he is so concerned that he despises the enacting of his own ordained religious ceremonies and practices while injustice is abroad:

> Your New Moon festivals and your appointed feasts
>   my soul hates.
> They have become a burden to me;
>   I am weary of bearing them.
> When you spread out your hands in prayer,

I will hide my eyes from you;
even if you offer many prayers,
    I will not listen.
Your hands are full of blood;
    wash and make yourselves clean.
Take your evil deeds
    out of my sight!
Stop doing wrong,
    learn to do right!
Seek justice,
    encourage the oppressed.
Defend the cause of the fatherless,
    plead the case of the widow.

(Isa. 1.14–17)

You oppress the righteous and take bribes
    and you deprive the poor of justice in the courts....
I hate, I despise your religious feasts;
    I cannot stand your assemblies.
Even though you bring me burnt offerings and grain
    offerings,
    I will not accept them.
Though you bring choice fellowship offerings,
    I will have no regard for them.
Away with the noise of your songs!
    I will not listen to the music of your harps.
But let justice roll on like a river,
    righteousness like a never-failing stream!

(Amos 5.12, 21–4)

The birth, life and death of Jesus Christ was also pregnant
with political implications even if the ministry of Jesus
was not in itself a political ministry (in the sense that Jesus
did not hold a formal political office). 'Kings will see you
and bow down, because of the Lord, who is faithful, the
Holy One of Israel, who has chosen you,' says God to his
suffering servant (Isa. 49.7). Mary the mother of Jesus

announces in regard to her coming child that God has 'brought down rulers from their thrones but has lifted up the humble' (Luke 1.52). Matthew records that the Magi came looking for the 'King of the Jews' and that King Herod understood Jesus' birth as a political threat (Matt. 2). The title 'Messiah' or 'Christ' that was given to Jesus during his ministry was a political title for it was synonymous with 'King of Israel' (John 1.49, Mark 8.29 and 14.61, 62). Indeed, Jesus was condemned to death on a political charge for it was only this that would have concerned the Roman occupiers: crucifixion was a Roman punishment that was reserved for slaves and political rebels amongst subject peoples. Indeed, John records that when Pilate tried to set Jesus free the Jews protested, 'If you let this man go, you are no friend of Caesar. Anyone who claims to be a king opposes Caesar' (John 19.12). Finally, despite the protests of the chief priests, the placard that went up on the cross read 'JESUS OF NAZARETH, THE KING OF THE JEWS' (John 19.19–21).

Now it is true that the kingdom that Jesus inaugurated was 'not of this world' (John 18.36) but we must take great care not to misunderstand this saying by interpreting it in terms of a split view of life. Jesus could not have meant that his kingdom had no implications for the politics of this world – this would have been to drive a wedge between the God of the New Testament and the God of the Old Testament who, as we have seen, is very much concerned with the politics of this world. Jesus meant that his kingdom does not derive from this world. In fact precisely the reverse is true: all political power that there is in the world derives from God in Christ (John 19.11). 'The authorities that exist have been established by God,' says Paul (Romans 13.1).

Jesus appears to make this same point in a particularly brilliant way on an occasion when the Herodians and Pharisees try to lead him into a political trap. This, I believe, is the most likely explanation of Mark 20.20–6.[1]

The question put to him is, should they pay taxes to Caesar? If Jesus were to answer 'no', then they could denounce him to the Romans for rebellion. If he had said 'yes', he would have been denounced by the people: the paying of taxes to their foreign occupiers was like an open sore to the nationalistic Jews.

While all those around him waited with bated breath, Jesus skilfully resolved the dilemma by asking for a coin. He then asked whose portrait was on the coin. When the Pharisees and Herodians answered that it was Caesar's, Jesus said, 'Give to Caesar what is Caesar's and to God what is God's' (Mark 20.25). The coin would have born both a picture of Caesar and an inscription which was a claim to divinity – to absolute authority. Jesus, like Paul, at one and the same time asserted that one should pay one's dues to an authority which derived its power from God for the keeping of law and order, and that no earthly power has absolute authority, only God.

We have seen, then, that the Bible is full of political content. We have also seen that all political power derives from God. It is to the God of the Bible that we therefore turn for our understanding of the meaning of justice. Indeed, Revelation 19.2 states that God's judgments are 'true and just'.

In Romans 2.11 we read 'God does not show favouritism'. As image-bearers of God our judgments must also be true, just, and impartial. An unjust judge in the Old Testament is one who does show partiality (Deut. 16.19). In Psalm 72 verses 1–4 we read:

Endow the king with your justice, O God,
    the royal son with your righteousness....
He will defend the afflicted among the people,
    and save the children of the needy;
    he will crush the oppressor.

A biblical understanding of justice is to do with defence

of the poor, the needy and the oppressed and the punishment of the oppressor.

In Exodus 21 verses 23–5 we read 'you are to take life for life, eye for eye, tooth for tooth, hand for hand, foot for foot, burn for burn, wound for wound.' These verses do not suggest a brutal way of revenge, as is often thought; rather they are about making sure that the punishment is not more severe than the wrong-doing warrants. The concern is to set limits on punishment so that it too is kept within the bounds of justice.

God is not only concerned that we deal justly with other humans but also with animals (Deut. 25.4) and even trees. 'Are trees of the fields people, that you should besiege them?' asks God (Deut. 20.19).

In his book *Thine is the Kingdom*, Paul Marshall, after surveying various texts regarding justice, concludes that justice in the Bible is to do with conforming to an order of 'right relations between God, persons and things,' and that it is about giving all creatures what is due to them.[2] Now, if as I have been arguing throughout this book, God calls creation to life in many dimensions then justice is about making it possible for all creatures to obey this calling. This, at least, is due to all of God's creatures. It is not 'just' that only the wealthy may seek emotional growth through psychotherapy or have access to adequate health care. It is not 'just' that only a comparatively small number of people have access to resources so that they may develop the aesthetic side of life. It is not 'just' that a few people have material prosperity while many more have barely enough on which to survive. The prophet Amos rails against the 'cows of Bashan' – the wealthy women of Samaria who revelled in luxury in their winter houses, summer houses and mansions while they oppressed the poor and crushed the needy (Amos 3.15, 4.1).

While some of us are denied access to the fullness of life that is due to them as God's creatures there is neither justice nor life for any of us. We are inseparably bound to each other. We are people in community. A biblical Hebraic term that is synonymous with 'life' in all of its dimensions is 'shalom'. 'Shalom' is 'peace, "wholeness", "soundness", hence health, wellbeing, prosperity ... good of any kind'.[3] The prophet Jeremiah laments that the people who have become 'rich and powerful and have grown fat and sleek' say 'Shalom, shalom when there is no shalom'. Why? Because there is no justice: 'they do not plead the case of the fatherless to win it, they do not defend the rights of the poor' (Jer. 5.27–8, 6.14).

We should also give our environment what is due to it by caring for it. Lake Ontario in Canada, once full of pure fresh drinking water, has signs near it warning of the danger to health not only of eating the polluted fish but also of swimming. Indeed, evidence of increasing pollution is to be found around the entire coast of the United States. Europe and our own country tell a similar story. Acid rain and a holed ozone layer is simply not giving the skies their due. For even the skies as creatures of God are called 'to proclaim the work of *God's* hands' (Ps. 19.1).

If justice in the Bible is about enabling all creatures to respond to God's call to life, all creatures are called to do justice.

> Lord, who may dwell in your sanctuary?
>   Who may live on your holy hill?
>
> He whose walk is blameless
>   and who does what is righteous,
> who speaks the truth from his heart
>   and has no slander on his tongue,
> who does his neighbour no wrong
>   and casts no slur on his fellow-man,
> who despises a vile man
>   but honours whose who fear the Lord,
> who keeps his oath

even when it hurts,
who lends his money without usury
    and does not accept a bribe against the innocent.

He who does these things
    will never be shaken.

(Ps. 15)

We who are parents, for example, should see to it that our children are given what is due to them, that they are cared for, loved and nurtured wisely. Then they will develop a strong sense of self, morally, emotionally and intellectually and so be well-equipped for life. Or if we are involved in health care then we are called to show no favouritism. We should play our part in making it possible for all to have access to adequate health care. We should remember that there is no sitting on the fence over this. To be human is to be political. If we are passive, our very passivity is in fact an 'active' aquiescence to the prevailing conditions.

As we have seen earlier, God calls us not only to nurture, grow and develop in all areas of life. He also calls and equips each of us for special vocations – to attend to and deepen particular areas. For example, an academic is called to deepen the intellectual dimension and an artist is called to deepen the aesthetic dimension. Justice also means that we enable a person to fulfil his or her special calling. We must ask if the disparity in incomes we find in our society is just. An artist has to live in virtual poverty (unless she 'prostitutes' her art by painting 'kitsch' pictures for a consumer market) whilst other callings, those usually associated with finance and big business, are rewarded to an inordinately high degree. (One can always detect the idolatry of a nation by how it rewards and therefore values certain callings above others.) Moreover, the 'poor artist' image gives art an unhealthy mystique by turning it into an ascetic vocation and elevating it above its rightful and ordinary place alongside other vocations in life.

Up until now we have not made a clear distinction between justice and politics. This we must now do. All of us are called to deal justly with all of God's creatures as we go about our daily lives, just as we are all called to be imaginative and playful in every area of life. Governments, however, are called to administer justice in society as a whole. They are called to relate different groups and individuals to each other in a 'just' way. They are to do this through law-making, public expenditure, administration, etc. Their aim should be to enable all creatures within their jurisdiction to fulfil their special vocations and receive the fullness of life. This is the task of government. It involves such matters as people's rights to a good job, freedom to worship, physical and emotional health, education, as well as to basic needs such as food, warmth and shelter. In short, it involves their right to 'shalom'.

I do not mean to imply that governments should give everyone what they want. Indeed this is impossible for they are not omnipotent. They cannot, for example, satisfy the road haulier's desire for a nation consisting entirely of four lane motorways as well as the desire of Sussex villagers for a 'rural paradise'. In practice, then, much of the work of government involves adjudicating where legitimate interests conflict.

Governing is what politics is all about. Some of us are called to be politicians in the way that some of us are called to be artists. As with art, to be called into politics is a divine calling as we can see from the evolution of government in the Bible.

The story of Cain and Abel appears to be about the origin of government. God firstly judges and delivers appropriate penalties on Cain for the murder of his brother and secondly protects Cain from further punishment by making a law that any who would harm him should also suffer penalties (Gen. 4.10–15). With Abraham we see God establishing a partnership with his human creatures in the area of government. He announces that Abraham, the chosen father of his special people 'will direct his [Abraham's] children and his household after him to keep the way of the Lord by doing what is right and just' (Gen. 18.19). Then he enters into a political argument with Abraham over the fate of Sodom and Gomorrah (Gen. 18.20ff).

Abraham was the patriarch of a nomadic clan and as such he performed many functions including those of prophet (Gen. 20.7), priest (Gen. 12.6ff, 22.9 – the building of altars and the offering of sacrifices was a priestly function), lawgiver and father. Later, after Israel had settled in her own land, the different functions in life were differentiated. In the book of Judges, Micah after first trying to appoint one of his sons as priest, finally appoints a Levite (Judg. 17). With Samuel we see the emergence of the function of prophet (1 Sam. 19.20ff), though Samuel also performed priestly functions (1 Sam. 3.1). We also see that first 'The Lord raised up judges' (Judg. 2.16) and later complied with Israel's request for a king (1 Sam. 11.12ff) not only to save Israel from its enemies but also to administer justice (Ps. 72.1–2).

Politics, then, has a divinely appointed authority in God's world, an authority which is distinct from all other authorities such as family, priest and prophet. If God calls us into politics then it is indeed a divine calling.

Because politics is one particular divine calling amongst others there are limits to the authority of political institutions. We have already mentioned an obvious one. Governments are not omnipotent: they should not claim absolute power. Jesus says this when he says 'Give to Caesar what is Caesar's and to God what is God's'. In recent history we have become painfully aware of what happens when the nation is turned into an idol. (See also Paul Tillich's words about nationalism in Chapter 2.)

Secondly, governments should not override the authority of other callings. In the Old Testament, political institutions had no authority over priests and prophets. Governments should not interfere, therefore, with such matters as how academic research should be carried out and for what purpose art should be done. They certainly should not use art for purposes of political propaganda (just as art should not be used for religious propaganda). Nor should they interfere with the religious beliefs in which children are brought up. But they should seek to maintain overall just interrelations among all institutions and among all creatures.

Although some of us are called into politics as a special vocation we are, as citizens in a democracy, all given the freedom to influence political decisions nationally and locally. Indeed as Christians we must take this responsibility seriously if we are to respond to God's call for justice in the world. There are a number of things we can do. We can campaign on issues; we can go on marches; we can sign petitions; we can write letters to members of parliament and councillors (this is more effective than people often think); we can join campaigning organisations such as the World Development Movement, Amnesty International, etc.; we can boycott such things as food imported from South Africa; we can raise issues and questions and set up discussion/action groups in our churches. This last point is very important: all our political action should be born out of intelligent, communal Christian reflection. Finally, we can vote for a particular political party.

Probably none of the political parties in this country would disagree, in principle anyway, that their task is to enable people to have the quality of life that the Bible calls 'shalom'. They might disagree about what is the most important aspect of shalom. The Right may focus on personal liberty, the Centre parties on democracy and tolerance and the Left on community and neighbourhood.

However, in reality these values are low on the agenda. It is quite obvious from listening to politicians that the chief concern of all the main parties is material prosperity. The Left, Right, and Centre parties all appear to share the assumption that material prosperity is the necessary condition for 'shalom'. To achieve material prosperity, then, is their real goal.

In the last few years there has been a general swing away from direct government action, towards letting market forces lead us onwards to this goal. However, all parties have their own, particular commitments.[4] 'Individualism' is the currently dominant belief of the Conservative party: Mrs Thatcher once said 'there is no such thing as society'. For her society is simply a collection of individuals (within families). Thus it is that the way to material prosperity is to allow individuals the freedom to maximise their potential to produce and also to consume what they have produced. Competition is natural and to be encouraged. 'Privatising' publicly owned companies is crucial. Competition will then encourage more efficiency and greater production and reduce prices. Profits will go to shareholders who will become more wealthy, and more people, by becoming shareholders, will share in this wealth. Some individuals will, however, become very wealthy. They will then be more able to employ the poor and pay for their work. Thus the poor will also benefit. They will then be able to afford to take responsibility for their own health care and other 'social services' without looking to the government.

The Conservative view accepts that there will always be inequality. It believes that human nature is such that if all individuals were given the same resources and opportunities, some would turn these into more while others would lose what they had. According to this view it is not a government task to interfere with human nature. It should be noted, however, that this belief is not so rigid that the government would not provide minimum welfare so that the poorest of the land are able to survive.

There does, however, seem to be something inherently unjust in the Conservative view. We are not all born with equal opportunity. We are born into existing social structures and with uneven wealth. Moreover, recent tax changes have led to even more inequality in income. I once played a game of Monopoly where instead of all the players starting off the game with the same amount of cash, we were all given different amounts and some players were given property at the outset. Hotels shot up in no time. It was virtually impossible for the poor players even to get a foothold in the game. Life is very like this version of Monopoly. Moreover, individualism linked with consumerism creates a greater tension between those who have and are able to 'maximise their potential' and those who have not and are unable.

If individualism is the central belief of the Conservative party, socialism or collectivism has been the central belief of the Labour party. According to this view, material prosperity for all will only be achieved by altering the present unjust social structures that keep the wealth and economic power perpetually in the hands of the few. That competition is natural or to be encouraged is a blatant lie. Rather, co-operation is natural and to be encouraged. However, only when we have solved our economic problems will co-operation be possible. If the Conservative party believes that we must be free to make money, the Labour party believes that we must have money to be free: 'If abundance is not possible then neither is socialism'.[5]

The state, then, must plan the economy in such a way as to guarantee greater equality of economic power and wealth. This can be achieved through the public ownership of companies, workers co-operatives and through such things as tax funded welfare, taxes on capital gains, death duties, etc.

The Labour party has in the past been committed to centralised state action to achieve redistribution of wealth. In recent years, however, it has come to believe that market forces must be allowed to play a role. Accordingly, the current debates within the party now centre on how much and in what way the government should interfere with the free market to produce more equality of wealth.

The policies of the centre parties differ in degree rather than in kind to those of Labour. The centre parties, however, are less dogmatic than the other two and they are committed to co-operation between parties.

Whatever critique we bring to bear on the policies of the biggest parties, the basic problem remains: their implicit idolatrous assumption that material prosperity is the goal of governments and the road to human happiness. Paul Marshall makes the interesting observation that the goal of material prosperity leads to what he calls a 'two-track' policy. One track is to pursue material prosperity, the other is to seek a way of 'mopping-up' the mess that results from this idolatry. For example, how to clean up the environment after industrial production has ravaged it; how to deal with the violence that ensues from unemployment and the sense of meaninglessness that goes with it; how to support those who are paid a comparative pittance because the market does not recognise the worth of their 'product'.[6]

If we stopped to ask if the pursuit of material prosperity brings us happiness, the answer, surely, is no. Recently, a colour supplement of one of the main national papers asked several 'successful' people precisely this question and every one of them spoke of their unhappiness. As Christians we understand why this is: idolising just one aspect of life leads to despair. Fulfilment comes about through opening up every area of our lives to God.

It must be said that the Green party does not have the

same narrow conception of material prosperity as the road to happiness as the other parties. In particular it has a more central concern for the environment. This is certainly a move in the right direction, but with our present electoral system (of non-proportional representation) unfortunately the Green party stands little chance of gaining power. Moreover, there appears to be a mixture of ideologies and beliefs within the party, including nature worship that has its roots in the Romantic movement of the nineteenth century and libertinism which wants such things as abortion on demand.

There is no Christian party to vote for or to join. Even if there was, the problems would not be over. We would all still argue over what 'Christian party' meant. We have to work with things as they are. This involves compromise. But compromise is not new to us. Many of us are not always entirely happy with church, for example, yet we do not all withdraw ourselves. We are called by God to political service in the 'fallen' political world as it is now.

8
... And God Made Room for Dinner Parties

The perspective that I have put forward in this book rests upon the belief that God created a multi-dimensional world. Our experience does indeed bear out this belief. Consider, for example, the distinctions we make in the sciences: physics, chemistry, biology, geography, psychology, aesthetics, economics, politics, ethics, theology and so on. Either we say that these distinctions are convenient and somewhat arbitrary inventions of the human mind, and that we impose them on an unformed reality for the purposes of analysis; or we say that the structure of creation itself gives rise to them. The first is a common enough philosophical view. But as Christians we must take the second one: the Christian doctrine of creation tells us that creation is an ordered diversity and that God creates this order, not we ourselves.

Creation, then, may be compared to a rich, but soiled, tapestry of many interwoven threads which God, and we in partnership with him, are re-making into something beautiful. We have looked at some of these threads and the part they play in the overall design. We have seen how our emotions and our faith interweave to form our sense of self and how our sense of self affects our relationship with others. We have seen that if imagination and play does not dance through this tapestry of creation then it will be a sorry, drab affair pleasing neither God nor humanity. We have seen how important it is that our faith-life changes and grows as we move through life.

And we have seen that unless the thread of justice is interwoven with every other thread in creation then the whole remains soiled. There are many more threads to creation that we have not had the time nor the expertise to examine, perhaps there are even more that are yet waiting to be discovered. This task will have to be left to others.

What I want to do in this final chapter is pick out and weave together again some threads, so to speak, of one very ordinary aspect of life – a dinner party. By doing this I hope to show how we can develop a method which will help us to think and act Christianly and redemptively in all areas of life.

We may think that a book about such an important matter as Christian faith should not finish on something as 'trivial' as a dinner party. Would it not be more appropriate to end on the more urgent theme of evangelism or social action for example? I suggest that such a reaction may well betray a sacred/secular split view of life which wants to relegate dinner parties to the secular area and out of God's sight. The question we must first ask is does God want us to have dinner parties and if so how are these to be pleasing to him?

The Bible has many references to feasts and festivals (Exod. 23.14ff; Num. 29.12; Deut. 16; Matt. 26.5, 17; Luke 14.12ff, etc.). In the Old Testament, God's great acts of deliverance were commemorated with feasts, as were certain times in the cycle of the seasons. In the New Testament we even find Jesus performing a miracle to save a wedding party from social disgrace (John 2). We find in the parable of the prodigal son and in the institution of the Lord's Supper a meal used as a symbol and celebration of reconciliation between God and humanity (Luke 15.22ff; Luke 22). The meal as a symbol for reconciliation and peace between hitherto estranged parties is very important. This morning I heard on the radio about a Russian mine sweeper that had its equipment torn away by fishing nets. It requested the help of a nearby British naval vessel which responded by sending out a helicopter to look for the equipment. The equipment was found. In the process of retrieving it, the Russian vessel took in a huge catch of fish. In order to show their gratitude they gave vast amounts of their catch to the British vessel. The British captain returned the gesture with a bottle of Scotch. Both captains exchanged best wishes for the New Year and went on their way. This marvellous spontaneous gesture of good will expressed in the exchange of food and drink would have been unheard of even a few years ago.

To return to the Bible: we read that after he was raised Jesus greeted his despondent disciples by preparing a meal on the sea-shore and inviting them to 'Come and have breakfast' (John 21.12).

All of these biblical feasts are to celebrate something – God's acts on our behalf, the regularity of seasons, a marriage, reconciliation and resurrection. But what about a feast for simple enjoyment of self and neighbour?

Deuteronomy 14.22ff is about the origin of tithing. God invites, even commands, the farming families among his people to give one tenth of their produce. They are not told to give this to the 'church' but they are to take their wine, grain and animals to a sanctuary chosen by God and there they are to have a big party. God suggests (but does not command) that they might like to invite the Levite to their party since he has no produce of his own. Every third year they are to invite the poor – 'the fatherless and the widows' – and the 'aliens' to the party. If the sanctuary was a long way away they were to sell their produce so that they could buy, on the spot, what they needed to make the party 'go': 'cattle, sheep, wine or other fermented drink, or anything you wish', says God. His simple command was that they 'rejoice'. 'Sanctuary feasts', says one commentator, 'meant feasting, revelry and strong drink' and this, says the text, is to take place 'in the presence of the Lord your God'![1]

God, then, wants his human creatures to have parties from time to time and he wants these to be fun. If we have a split view of life we may think that the only valid reason to hold a dinner party is as a means for evangelism. However, according to the biblical view, it would seem that if there is to be any doubt about the validity of a Christian dinner party, it is not over whether it lacks an evangelistic thrust, but whether it is joyful enough to be pleasing to God!

So let us see what is involved in making a dinner party a joyful response to God. A good (God-pleasing) dinner party involves more than culinary ingredients, it involves a righteous handling of all of the 'ingredients' of God's creation.

Firstly, there is the question of whom to invite. Should it be friends? Then it will be a relaxing time and I can be myself. But maybe it would be better to invite a few people who don't know each other very well. I've lived in this street for three years now and still do not know the doctor and his wife or the couple on the corner and they don't seem to know each other either. It would be harder work, we may not hit it off, but maybe it is a risk worth taking; if I get to know a few people better I'd feel more at home here. I'd have more of a sense of community. Maybe I'll invite some of each group – that way I'll get the best of both worlds. Yet in my experience having a dinner party where some of the guests are friends and some strangers doesn't seem to work well: the ones who know each other tend to be too familiar and the strangers feel uneasy and excluded. I'll take the plunge and go for neighbours not friends.

But how many people shall I invite? How many knives and forks, chairs and crockery do I have? Moreover, I don't want to spend the whole of Saturday cooking. What would be the best number so that the conversation doesn't split up into separate conversations? Maybe it would be better if it did. This would mean less work for me to keep everything going and I could slip away and attend to the food. What about the space? it's only a small room and the table isn't that big. It's cosy, six people will do well, any more and it will seem overcrowded. I wonder how it would be best to seat people, to make the conversation go well?

What should we eat? I know one of the guests is a vegetarian; she says it's for health reasons, because all the hormone chemicals are bad for us. I'll make a vegetable dish and I'll buy all the vegetables from the organic food shop. They taste better than ordinary vegetables. They will cost a little more, but if the guests bring wine I can save a bit on that. I must make sure that I buy sufficient so that everyone has enough to eat. I hope they all turn up on time, it is crucial that this particular dish is eaten as soon as it is cooked.

Vegetarian dishes often seem to me to be somewhat bland. I must choose a recipe that not only tastes good but also looks good. Also, I would like to introduce the guests to something that they probably have not had before. I've a few specialities up my sleeve that I can draw from.

Should we say grace? It would be a good opportunity to let them all know that I am a Christian. It would also be an opportunity to draw attention to the fact that many people do not themselves have enough to eat let alone are able invite others to share a meal. But then again this might cause tensions. One of the guests may have had a bad experience with religion, or one of them might be an atheist. I don't want to make them feel uncomfortable by including them in a ritual that may only be meaningful to me. It is more important for them and me to feel as relaxed as possible. I'd rather let the whole dinner party be an expression of the kind of God I worship. If it is a joyful event, it will take its place alongside the rest of creation in 'declaring the glory of God' (Ps. 19).

Now what I have described above is very, even embarrassingly, ordinary. And this is precisely the point. It is in going about our everyday lives that we have to do with God. We do not have to do theology to make contact with God nor do we have to retreat to an inner pious sanctuary, nor do we only come into God's presence in church. God is truly Emmanuel – with us in our everyday activities. Moreover, whatever we do we are to 'do it all for the glory of God' (1 Cor. 10.31). In the case of a dinner party, as we have seen, glory is given to God if it is a joyful occasion.

Now let us analyse what is involved in making our dinner party give glory to God. As well as the physical objects involved we had to consider numbers – of people, chairs, space, etc. We had to consider the psychological relationships and communication within the group. We thought of the nutritional or biological value of the food. We had to make economic decisions about it and consider fairness. We also thought of fairness or justice in a larger context – that of a world in which so many people have no chance at all of holding a joyful festival but hardly survive from day to day on the meagre amounts of food that come their way. An important dimension of the meal is the aesthetic dimension – we wanted the food to look and taste good. We also wanted the table to be set out in a pleasing way. Cracked cups for the wine would have been disappointing. We wanted to bring in an element of education into the meal – learning something new. A dimension of trust or commitment was involved – that the guests would arrive as agreed. And lastly a dimension of faith was involved as we wrestled with the decision concerning the saying of grace.

We may also learn from our dinner party how interwoven is the fabric of creation. One dimension of life affects another. For a dinner party to be the joyous event it is called to be, careful consideration is needed to be given to all dimensions. For example: the numbers of guests and the seating arrangements helps to determine the ease of conversation. The visual setting and imaginative presentation of the food either increases joy or detracts from it. If the guests were to arrive late, trust would be broken and bad feelings would arise.

Can this analysis of a dinner party help us to go about our Christian task in other areas of life? I think that it can. Let us pinpoint the essential components. Firstly, we ask of the thing, event or institution that we are considering what is it called to be and do in God's world? How is it a service of love to God and creation? Secondly, we think of all the other dimensions of creation that are involved. Thirdly, we consider how we might 'open up' or redeem all of these dimensions so that the whole may achieve its God-ordained, life-giving function.

When I teach people this method I ask them to choose a particular institution for analysis. I suggest that someone chooses a particular hospital they know, another a school, another a business. Take a hospital for example, its place in God's world is for the restoration of bodily health. As with the dinner party, in order to fulfil this function many other dimensions of creation are involved. The hospital needs to have adequate financial resources so that it can afford the latest technology. It also needs to be sensitive to the emotional aspect of physical health. There has been a tendency in western medicine to underplay this aspect. Again, this is because our western view of human nature tends to split mind from body. Patients, therefore, have often been regarded not as whole people with emotions and bodies inseparably bound but rather their bodies have been seen as separate, autonomous possessions, 'your body needs healing' rather than 'you need healing' captures this view.

The aesthetic dimension of the hospital is also crucial. I have already shown in an earlier chapter how important this is in helping a person feel human and cared for. The hospital architecture too tells us how we are thought of.

Does the building tell us that efficiency is the overriding aspect and that we are to be compared with battery hens, or is there an element of playfulness and imagination in the design which tells us that we are human beings created in God's image?

The element of trust is of great importance in a hospital. Can we trust that the surgeons and nurses are not so tired by overwork that they are likely to make mistakes? Do we know that they have been well taught in medical practice, that their diagnosis or analysis of our disorders is accurate? What about numbers and space? Does overcrowding create practical problems and lead to emotional distress? Then there is the element of justice. Is it 'just' that those who are financially well off have access to better, faster health care than others? Is it 'just' that nursing is one of the lowest paid professions in our country? What about the social side of life in a hospital? Are patients shown dignity and respect by the medical staff and are the medical staff treated with dignity and respect by the patients?

Economics, justice, aesthetics, trust, numbers, space, analysis, education, emotions, the social aspect – these are just some of the God-given dimensions of life that run through all of creation. By careful consideration of these we may begin to see how a hospital may live up to its divine calling to be a place of healing. We can do the same kind of analysis with a school, with a business or indeed with any anything in creation.

Indeed, we are called to the task of thinking through and, where we have the power, actively changing, everything in our culture so that it brings glory to God and life to ourselves and our neighbour. By doing just this we do indeed 'prepare the way for the Lord' (Isa. 40.3).

I began this book by saying that the concern to be thoroughly Christian in everything we do entails that we start with our own lives as we live them now. We should not lose sight of this. I would, therefore like to finish this chapter and this book in the way that it started. Then I asked you to draw a tree. I asked you to write down the trunk of the tree in a short phrase what you believed the heart of the gospel message to be. I asked you to draw seven branches to represent the major areas and concerns of your life. I then asked you to consider how the gospel as you understand it affects these areas of your life. Where you were clear about this I asked you to join the trunk to the tree. Where you were unclear I asked you to use a dotted line. Where you could find no connection I asked you to leave the branch hanging in mid-air. Now, I ask you to draw another tree and to repeat the whole process. If you can now join up more of the branches to the trunk of the tree, i.e. if you are now more able to see how you may live the whole of your life more Christianly, then this book will have achieved its purpose.

Notes

1. Sacred and Secular Splits

1 Peter Anderson, 'Pop Goes the Gospel', *Evangelism Today* (October, 1981).

2 Ernest Becker, *The Denial of Death* (New York: Macmillan, 1973), p.26.

3 Edward Bach, *Heal Thyself* (1937; Saffron Walden: Daniel, 1988), p.10.

4 See James B. Nelson, *Embodiment: An Approach to Sexuality and Christian theology* (London: SPCK, 1979), p.47.

5 Susan Griffin, *Pornography and Silence* (New York: Harper and Row, 1981; London: Women's Press, 1981). I have summarised her argument in my essay on pornography in *Dark Glasses*, eds. Steve Shaw and Sue Plater (London: Marc Europe, 1987), p.22.

6 A. J. Ayer, *Language, Truth and Logic* (London: Gollancz, 1936; Harmondsworth: Penguin, 1971), p.153.

7 Karl Stern, *The Flight from Woman* (London: Allen and Unwin, 1966), p.76.

8 *Phaedo*, paras 66, 67.

9 *Phaedo*, para 67.

10 L. E. Keck, *Paul and his Letters* (Philadelphia: Fortress Press, 1979), p.185.

11 G. E. Ladd, *The Pattern of New Testament Truth* (Grand Rapids: Eerdmans, 1968), p.15.

2. Faith as Ultimate Concern

1 *The Four Families* (National Film Board, 1959). My colleagues Brian Walsh and Richard Middleton refer to this film to make a similar point in *The Transforming Vision: Shaping a Christian World View*, p.17.

2 James Fowler, *Stages of Faith: The Psychology of Human Development and the Quest for Meaning* (New York: Harper and Row, 1981), p.4.

3 Paul Tillich, *The Dynamics of Faith* (New York: Harper and Row, 1957), p.1.

4 The Canadian theologian Wilfred Cantwell-Smith has traced historically the evolution of the meaning of the word 'belief' and its relationship to faith in *Faith and Belief* (New Jersey: Princeton University Press, 1979).

5 One of the best discussions of this subject is to be found in Michael Polanyi, *Personal Knowledge* (Chicago: University of Chicago Press, 1962). See also John Hick, *Faith and Knowledge* (Cleveland, Ohio: Collins, 1978).

3. Christ – Our Ultimate Concern

1 I have already explained in Chapter 2 how a myth is a story about the ultimate meaning of life and how its truth is grasped by faith.

2 I believe that this is the position taken by the theologians Don Cupitt and John Hick. See my M.Phil. thesis: *The Continuity of John Hick's Thought* (Toronto: Institute for Christian Studies, 1985).

3 Calvin Seerveld, *Rainbows for the Fallen World*, p.53.

4   Walsh and Middleton in *The Transforming Vision*,
    pp.55–56.
5   G. von Rad, *Old Testament Theology* Vol. 1 (London: SCM Press, 1975), p.422.
6   That the Christian life is to be seen as spiritual warfare
    is well argued by Andrew Walker in *Enemy Territory: The Christian Struggle for the Modern World*.
7   See my essay on pornography in *Dark Glasses* (London: Marc Europe, 1987).
8   See H. Fernhout, *Man: The Image and the Glory of God* (Toronto: AACS).
9   Gen. 1.15. See also Heb. 1.3.

4. And God Made Room for the Self

1   Erich Fromm, *The Art of Loving* (1957; London: Allen and Unwin, 1985), p.53.
2   James B. Nelson, *Embodiment: An Approach to Sexuality and Christian Theology* (London: SPCK, 1979), p.83. St Augustine defined sin precisely in these terms.
3   This was initiated by Murray White, the head teacher of Kings Hedges primary school, Cambridge.
4   As James Olthuis notes in 'Sense and Non-sense of Self' (*Vanguard*, May/June 1979), given the fact that as yet a fully Christian approach to psychotherapy has not been clearly worked out, one has to take what is available. Indeed, as long as a therapist or support group respect a person's beliefs it is not essential that they share these beliefs. This is not to deny that the various schools of psychotherapy have 'religious' presuppositions nor that beliefs and feelings are not intimately connected. It simply recognises that the *focus* of therapy is on feelings and not on faith.

5. ... And God Made Room for Style, Imagination and Play

1 Traditionally, aesthetics has been understood to be about the appreciation of beauty. This is not the view I put forward in this chapter. My view of aesthetics is based on the original work of the Christian aesthetician Calvin Seerveld. See Calvin Seerveld's book *Rainbows for the Fallen World* for a full presentation of his position.

2 L. Bradshaw Fray *et al.*, *At Work and Play* (Ontario: Paideia Press, 1986), p.53.

3 Calvin Seerveld, *Rainbows for the Fallen World*, pp.63–6.

4 *Sword and Trowel*, newsletter of the Metropolitan Tabernacle (February 1985), pp.13–14.

6. ... And God Made Room for Faith Development

1 James W. Fowler, *Stages of Faith: The Psychology of Human Development and the Quest for Meaning*.

2 Ibid., pp.146–7.

3 Ibid., p.181.

7. ... And God Made Room for Justice

1 This is the view taken by the New Testament theologian Alan Richardson in *The Political Christ* (London: SCM Press, 1973), p.47.

2 Paul Marshall, *Thine is the Kingdom*, p.55.

3 The article on 'Peace' in the *Hastings Dictionary of the Bible* (Edinburgh: T. & T. Clark, 8th imp. 1906).

4 See the chapter on 'Ideology' in H. Drucker *et al.* (eds.), *Development in British Politics 2* (London:

Macmillan, 1986), pp.8ff.

5   In *Socialism* (Bantam, 1973), p.425.

6   *Thine is the Kingdom*, p.104.

8. ... And God Made Room for Dinner Parties

1   Peake's *Commentary on the Bible*, p.277.

Select Bibliography

John Chaplin *et al.*, *An Introduction to a Christian World View* (The Open Christian College, 1986. Available from Carol Holliday, 83 Brampton Rd, Cambridge CB1 3HJ).

Os Guinness, *The Gravedigger File* (London: Hodder and Stoughton, 1983).

Arthur F. Holmes, *Contours of a Christian World View* (Grand Rapids: Eerdmans, 1983; Leicester: IVP, 1983).

Andrew Kirk, *A New World Coming: A Fresh Look at the Gospel for Today* (Basingstoke: Marshall Morgan and Scott, 1983).

Paul Marshall, *Thine is the Kingdom* (Basingstoke: Marshalls, 1984).

Lesslie Newbiggin, *Foolishness to the Greeks* (London: SPCK, 1986).

H. Richard Niebuhr, *Christ and Culture* (New York: Harper and Row, 1951).

Calvin Seerveld, *Rainbows for the Fallen World* (Toronto: Tuppence Press, 1980; Greenbelt Festivals, 1988).

James Sire, *The Universe Next Door* 2nd edition (Leicester: Inter-Varsity Press, 1988).

Alan Storkey, *A Christian Social Perspective* (Leicester: IVP, 1979).

Andrew Walker, *Enemy Territory: The Christian Struggle for the Modern World* (London: Hodder and Stoughton, 1987).

Brian J. Walsh and J. Richard Middleton, *The Transforming Vision* (Illinois: IVP, 1984).

Albert Wolters, *Creation Regained* (Grand Rapids: Eerdmans, 1985; Leicester: IVP, 1986).

Survivor:
A Tribute to Cliff

Tony Jasper

Tributes from celebrities as diverse as Sting and Billy Graham, Cilla Black and the Archbishop of Canterbury are included in this special anniversary publication to mark Cliff Richard's astonishingly successful thirty years in the music business. In this most competitive of all businesses, where big names fall as quickly as they rise, Cliff has outlived them all: '.... *the Liverpool sound, the mass of groups, flower power, metal, junk, punks, the disco scene, the technical bods, computer music, you name it he's stayed in there. He's a survivor*', Mickie Most.

Hardback 018674

Valeri Barinov:
The Trumpet Call

Lorna Bourdeaux

Foreword by Cliff Richard
Introduction by
The Rt Hon. David Steel MP

The profoundly moving story of talented Russian musician, Valeri Barinov, whose imprisonment aroused worldwide condemnation of Soviet persecution.

Pocket paperback 012978

Art in Question

Tim Dean & David Porter (Eds.)

The 1984 London Lectures in Contemporary Christianity covered the definition, justification and purpose of art from a Christian perspective. Contributors include Graham Birtwistle, Ruth Etchells and Murray Watts.

Trade paperback 013214

Ex–Machina

25 Original Sketches

David Lee

A welcome collection of new drama sketches – with a hard edge. Some are for adults, some for children, some for church services and missions, some for performing in front of Sainsbury's. The sketches use dramatic techniques as diverse as stand-up comedy, dance, puppetry ... even a four-part rap. All have been written to communicate the Christian faith with the style and humour of the 1990's.

Pocket paperback 018348

Seeing in the Dark

Philip Yancey

Philip Yancey tackles the crisis of faith that occurs when God seems to leave us to face our struggles alone. When we ask for guidance and it is not given; when we pray for healing and it is not granted; when we seek God's blessing and then lose the very thing we cherish – what is happening? Is God silent? Capricious? Or hiding from us? Drawing on real life examples with which we are all familiar, Philip Yancey searches for answers to questions which stir inside many Christians, yet which few would ever ask aloud.

Trade paperback 018682

Rich Christians,
Poor Christians

Monica Hill

An expansive book, rich with experiences of Christianity from all parts of the worldwide church. Having drawn from the spirutal life and health of the church worldwide, Monica Hill seeks to identify the underlying principles of renewal and encourages us to adapt these to our own individual situations.

Pocket paperback 018984

Two Million
Silent Killings

The Truth About Abortion

Dr Margaret White

A striking and thorough investigation into abortion. GP Margaret White exposes the deliberate attempt to confuse the public over the issue of abortion and replies to the pro-abortionists' arguments in terms of God's basic rules for health and life. Illustrated.

Trade paperback 014024

Journey Towards Holiness

A way of living for God's nation

Alan Kreider

Holiness is about *life*; it is about finding new ways of making God's kingdom a distinctive and visible social reality. Surveying the biblical history of God's working in the world, Alan Kreider defined what being his holy nation means for us today.

Trade paperback 013621

Aids and the Positive Alternatives

Dr Margaret White

A forthright, informed book advocating positive lifestyles and choices based on Christian values, yet written with compassion and understanding. From sound medical information to the theological issues raised by Aids, Dr White focuses on the whole of a person's emotional well-being.

I Will Heal Their Land

God's work in
South Africa today

Eileen Vincent

An exciting account of God's work in South Africa from which the church at home can learn important lessons to hastenthe day of its own spiritual revival.

Pocket paperback 013311

And If It's True?

Peter Vardy

In the tradition of *Mere Christianity* and *God of Surprises*, *And If It's True?* is a clear, compelling and reasoned account of the challenge of personal faith. Exploring the 'big' questions which we all have to face – love, commitment, mabition, suffering, death – *And If It's True?* uncovers the *real* vision that lies at the heart of Christianity.

Trade paperback 017635

Spirituality
at Street Level

Ray Mayhew

Spirituality at Street Level is a working-out of every Christian of the consequences of entry into the spiritual life of Christ. This is a radical and life-changing move: it means living by the beatitudes with discipline and holiness, in community with each other, and seeking to join our human spirit with the Holy Spirit at work in the world.

Trade paperback 016094

What Kind of Country?

David Alton

Taking the primary issues of the day, which affect us as individuals, communities and as a country and part of the human race with responsibilities for one another, David Alton shows the way to a positive Christian and creative response.

Trade paperback 016124